KINGS OF FRIDAY NIGHT
THE LINCOLNS

A. J. B. Johnston

Foreword by John MacLachlan Gray
Afterword by Frank MacKay

NIMBUS
PUBLISHING
—— NIMBUS.CA ——

Nimbus Publishing Limited
3660 Strawberry Hill Street, Halifax, NS, B3K 5A9
(902) 455-4286 nimbus.ca

Printed and bound in Canada

NB1459

Editor: Barry Norris
Cover design: Colin Smith
Interior design: Jenn Embree
Cover images: *The Lincolns, circa 1963. Left to right: Layne Francis, Lee Taylor, Frank MacKay, Rod Norrie, Brian Chisholm, Frank Mumford.* (**PRIDHAM STUDIO**); *Frank MacKay.* (**DOUG HILTZ**)
Back cover: *The Lincolns, circa 1968. Front to back: Rod Norrie (drums), Frank MacKay (vocals), Don Muir (bass), Layne Francis (saxophone), Frank Mumford (guitar), John MacLachlan Gray (organ).* (**DALHOUSIE UNIVERSITY ARCHIVES**)

Library and Archives Canada Cataloguing in Publication

Title: Kings of Friday night : the Lincolns / A. J. B. Johnston ; foreword by John MacLachlan Gray ; afterword by Frank MacKay.
Names: Johnston, A. J. B. (Andrew John Bayly)
Identifiers: Canadiana (print) 20200170163 | Canadiana (ebook) 20200170651 | ISBN 9781771088480 (softcover) | ISBN 9781771088497 (HTML)
Subjects: LCSH: Lincolns (Musical group : Truro, N.S.) | LCSH: Rock groups—Nova Scotia—Biography. | LCSH: Rock musicians—Nova Scotia—Biography.
Classification: LCC ML421.L742 J72 2020 | DDC 782.421640922—dc23

Canada Council   Conseil des arts
for the Arts   du Canada

NOVA SCOTIA

Nimbus Publishing acknowledges the financial support for its publishing activities from the Government of Canada, the Canada Council for the Arts, and from the Province of Nova Scotia. We are pleased to work in partnership with the Province of Nova Scotia to develop and promote our creative industries for the benefit of all Nova Scotians.

OTHER BOOKS BY A. J. B. JOHNSTON

Something True
The Hat
Thomas, A Secret Life (Thomas Pichon Novel No. 1)
The Maze (Thomas Pichon Novel No. 2)
Crossings (Thomas Pichon Novel No. 3)

Ancient Land, New Land
Grand Pré: Landscape for the World
Louisbourg: Past, Present, Future
N'in na L'nu: The Mi'kmaq of Prince Edward Island
N'in na L'nu : Les Mi'kmaq de l'Ile du Prince-Édouard
Endgame 1758: The Promise, the Glory, and the Despair of Louisbourg's Last Decade
1758: La finale, promesses, splendeur, et désolation
Grand-Pré, Heart of Acadie / Grand-Pré, Coeur de l'Acadie
Storied Shores: St. Peter's, Isle Madame, and Chapel Island
Control and Order: French Colonial Louisbourg
Life and Religion at Louisbourg
Tracks Across the Landscape
Louisbourg: The Phoenix Fortress
Louisbourg : Reflets d'une époque
Louisbourg: An 18th-Century Town
The Summer of 1744 / L'été de 1744
From the Hearth: Recipes from the Fortress of Louisbourg
Defending Halifax, Ordnance, 1825–1906

For the makers and lovers of live music—everywhere, in all its forms—
and to the memory of departed Lincolns
Peter Harris, Lee Taylor, Brian Chisholm, Frank Mumford,
and Frank MacKay

TABLE OF CONTENTS

Foreword

FRANK

When Beverlee and I arrived in Truro for the Lincolns reunion in September 2018, I didn't know what to expect and worried that it could possibly be a shit show.

We hadn't played together for forty years, yet we were going to perform heaven knows how many numbers, with one rehearsal and one sound check.

It promised to be a recipe for disaster.

But that's not what happened. The players came prepared. We listened to one another. We seemed to know exactly what was required of us. A spirit of generosity prevailed—especially toward the playwright-novelist who once thought he was a musician.

All because Frank MacKay was leading the band.

It made for an amazing two nights, for all kinds of reasons— ask anyone who was there. But for me, going home to Truro a half-century after having left (excepting funerals), the experience was some sort of a revelation.

I'll get back to that, but now that Frank (and The Lincolns) have "left the building," I'd like to devote a few words to that remarkable guy.

When I first got to know Frank, we were both chubby loners in high school—a closeted gay teen (not a thing then) and a lazy underachiever with undiagnosed ADD (not a thing, either.)

I don't remember when or how, but Frank introduced me to soul music. He worked behind the counter in a tiny grocery with a bell on the door, in the front of a house on Arthur Street. And in the spaces between customers (sometimes lasting an hour), we'd sit in the living room listening to his records played on a 1960s walnut veneer console that looked like a dresser: Wilson Pickett, Solomon Burke, Don Covay, Otis Redding, and his idol at the time, Ray Charles.

Already Frank was known locally for his extraordinary voice. I remember seeing him with The Corvettes, at about fifteen, lying on the floor bellowing into the mic. He was in a league of his own even back then. Trying to harmonize with Frank, I felt like a mouse squeaking in the background.

Built like an opera singer, he had a massive forehead and chest (natural resonators) and near-perfect pitch; and he radiated an energy—think Fats Domino, Billy Stewart, Jackie Gleason for that matter—that dominated the stage without physical effort. And what a charmer.

Offstage, however, he was more complicated.

Frank read a lot but pretended not to. He had a remoteness to him. And he could be prickly. During dances at the IGA Hall, anyone who requested a Monkees tune at a school dance was in for a withering blast. One-to-one, though, he was funny, curious, and smart—the kind of guy you wanted to hang around with.

I joined The Lincolns in 1966 while attending Mount Allison University. By then, the band was playing Fridays at the Legion, to crowds of seven hundred and up. (On Saturdays, the Lord's Day Act kicked in at eleven thirty to clear the hall.)

Many an Upper Canadian star came to grief trying to play Truro on a Friday night. On later trips to hear music in Montreal, when I mentioned to a player that I played with The Lincolns, the inevitable response was a version of: "Oh yeah? Still have Truro sewn up?"

When I joined up, the band contained, among others, a blond hunk, a boy-next-door, a beat hipster, and MacKay—among The Lincolns he was called MacKay to distinguish him from guitarist Frank Mumford. By then, Frank had evolved into a huge, intimidating, hairy presence who might have reminded people of a caveman, wearing a fur bathing suit and carrying a club.

In 2018 he and I picked up just where we'd left off a few years before—talking about music and life, driving around in his purple Cougar with the flip-up headlights. All Truro heaved a sigh of relief when he quit driving; when Frank once picked me up in Sackville for a gig, my landlady went rigid with terror. Sometimes he would drive me the ninety miles to Mount A so that we could continue talking about whatever was on our minds.

When next we met, it was in Ottawa in 1981, thirteen years after I'd left the band. Frank had joined the cast of *Rock and Roll*—which would go on to become a feature video called *King of Friday Night*—in the role of Parker: the fat, ornery kid with a killer voice. (In retrospect, I realize that Parker was a cross between Frank and me.)

I cast him with no audition. I had never seen him act but had observed his wicked ability to imitate other people, together with his command of an audience. And I knew voice projection would not be an issue. In any case, I had no Plan B—it just had to be him.

When he arrived at the National Arts Centre, we just picked up where we left off.

By then, he was what one would call a heavy drinker. He had always been fond of beer in quantity (weren't we all?), but now it was consecutive Double D (dark rum) and O (orange juice) cocktails—

the server at the Lord Elgin Hotel didn't have to ask. Still, the man shaped up on demand, a real pro. Never late for rehearsal, knew his lines early, and performed brilliantly throughout a long run and two tours. Theatre means repetition night after night, but Frank never became stale, any more than he did singing "Knock On Wood" for the thousandth time.

So, when I cast the role of Charlie Chamberlain in *Don Messer's Jubilee* [a musical that paid tribute to the long-running and highly popular nationwide TV show of the 1950s and 1960s], it was the easiest decision I ever made. And, of course, when we got together in Halifax in 1984, we just picked up where we left off.

Except that Frank had undergone a remarkable transformation. He had quit drinking entirely. He had lost maybe fifty pounds. He was running five miles a day. But more than that, he had acquired a sweet, generous, almost saintly disposition.

Where on earth did he find the inner strength to do that? I still don't know, and I am still in awe.

Don't get me wrong—I always loved Frank. And when he was crabby, he made me laugh. (If you were a Neil Young fan, best stand clear.) But now it seemed as though a great weight had been lifted from his shoulders. He didn't sing to win over an audience anymore, he sang because he loved to sing. I had the sense that he was sharing a gift—that even with no audience, he would sing anyway.

Without bringing religion into it (and he sure didn't), it was as though Frank had seen, I dunno, some sort of light. I can't imagine what kind of light he saw, but I am certain that he saw it while singing.

In *Don Messer*, as always, he was brilliant. Through three productions and a Canadian tour, he anchored the cast so that even McGinty, a very Irish band, maintained a behavioural standard when MacKay was around.

That was the pattern between Frank and me: long-term gigs with long periods in between, then we just picked up where we left off. And that is exactly what happened with The Lincolns Reunion at the Legion Hall in 2018.

In Barry Ryan's basement studio and onstage, Frank was the maestro, directing the band in dozens of subtle ways without for one moment losing contact with the audience. He was like an energy field, spinning about the stage, drawing everybody in.

And while playing "Danny Boy," Frank's signature piece, I started to get it.

With "Danny Boy," his singing combined a soul/gospel sensibility with the keening high notes of a Scottish tenor. In other words, his singing was an expression of Scottish-Black culture. A kid named MacKay, descended from coal miners, who idolized Ray Charles.

Which leads me to the role of The Lincolns in the town of Truro.

Looking back, Truro in the 1960s was a collection of solitudes—East End, West End, the Island, Black, Mi'kmaw, Protestant, Catholic, Syrian, Lebanese—living in tight circles that rarely overlapped. In fact, I can think of only one occasion on which these diverse groups gathered under one roof: at The Lincolns dance on Friday night, when everyone danced to Black music, played by a group of white guys, with a charismatic Celtic soul singer up front.

While in Truro, Beverlee and I drove around to look at my old haunts. The Island I remembered had disappeared, as had Ford Street. In their place was a multiracial community of well-kept homes. We walked up Prince to Inglis Street and met servers and clerks and pedestrians, and it became abundantly clear that Truro is a different town now.

I can't help but think that The Lincolns had something to do with that.

In the unlikely event that the town ever feels the need for another monument, I'd love to see, rather than some historical luminary, a statue of Frank MacKay in a baseball cap, mic in hand, nailing a power note for one last chorus of "Danny Boy."

John MacLachlan Gray
Organist with The Lincolns, 1966–68

Overture

BACK IN THE DAY

oming along Brunswick Street from my West End home, I could hear the music pulsating down the block. It was an audio magnet drawing me to its source, the weekly dance that was the talk of the town. Well, the talk of its young people, those who were growing up in the mid-1960s. Our parents' music—the easy listening sounds of Mantovani, Guy Lombardo, and Irving Berlin—was not what we wanted. We wanted music to make our feet and hips move, and maybe our hair stand up. We wanted something with a pronounced beat. We wanted rock 'n' roll. And in Truro, Nova Scotia, more than anything else, that meant the town's very own number one band, The Lincolns.

Ever louder the sound grew the closer I got to the Colchester Legion. Yet it was still dulled, flattened by the building's thick brick walls. And by the hum of a hundred conversations. For many others were also hurrying to the same place I was. We all had but one thought: to get inside Nova Scotia's most electrifying dance hall.

Up the entrance steps I went, three warm quarters clutched in my hand. With each stride, the music climbed in intensity.

Finally, I recognized the song I'd not deciphered outside. It was a soul number I'd heard on the radio, every bit as powerful as the original. No—better, because it was being performed in this very building.

Seventy-five cents paid, and at last through the jumble of people in the foyer, I shouldered my way into the main hall. Hundreds of dancers crowded the floor, and beyond, onstage, through the smoke and sweat, was the band. I counted seven players. No, not quite. Six had instruments, and there was an arm-pumping singer whose voice could cut through steel. Anchored by the drums, with rhythm in the guitars and the horns taking off, an organ was lifting the roof while the soulful singer lit the night. It was incredibly tight.

Never before had I heard or seen anything like it. The band—The Lincolns—was shaking the foundations of Legion Branch No. 26 as close to a thousand dancers and watchers grooved along. All memory of junior high record hops disappeared. So too did listening to namby-pamby 45s like "Rhythm of the Rain" in the knotty pine–panelled basements of my friends' parents. This was something else. It was intense. Alive! More exciting than anything I'd ever imagined.

I was no longer in the staid old town of my birth, in Nothing-Ever-Happens-Here, Nova Scotia, population twelve thousand. Somehow, a mere twenty-minute walk from my house was this totally alternate Truro. Here was a world that had nothing to do with my hometown's usual claims to fame—railway hub, thousand-acre Victoria Park, and source of Stanfield's underwear. This was a Truro that sounded like...I couldn't guess: Memphis, maybe? Because I knew that was where Stax Records was based, and the guys up onstage were pumping out a soulful sound worthy of comparison.

It was a blast.

The epiphany happened more than fifty years ago, yet I still recall the first time I entered the realm of The Lincolns, Truro's legendary "kings of Friday night." The memory is as vivid as if it were yesterday. The encounter left me more than a little transformed and transfixed.

The funny thing is that I can't recall if I shared that first exposure to The Lincolns with a friend or if I went to the Legion all by myself. Nor do I remember the month or year—such details hardly seemed to matter. There was something much bigger at play that night: a life force I had never before heard, seen, or felt. Its intensity illuminated the hall and everyone in it.

If I had to guess, I'd say that first exposure to The Lincolns occurred in the fall of 1965. If so, I was in Grade 10, not far away from turning sixteen. Or maybe it was 1966, me in Grade 11 and a year older. Whenever it was, I now understand that it was the absolute best time to encounter the distinctive music of the famous Truro band. My hormones were regularly in play, with all the angst and longing that entailed. Thankfully—gratefully—the songs The Lincolns played were a perfect fit. Not just for me, but for thousands of other young Nova Scotians as well. That was because the band's repertoire was not just any old rock 'n' roll. More than anything it was soul and rhythm and blues, the kind of music that simultaneously stirred and soothed body and heart.

Today, I'd say going to a Lincolns dance was a rite of passage. At the time, I'd have said I was simply—finally!—growing up. *Hey Jay, this is a different world! What do you think? Isn't it great?* I know I was far from unique. Many before and after had much the same experience at their first encounter with The Lincolns. For me, it was at the Truro Legion. Before 1965, it had happened

The author (right) and best friend, Craig Stanfield, on Smith Avenue, Truro, 1966; in the background is the house in which Lincoln Don Muir grew up.
(VICTORIA STANFIELD DYMOND)

at other Colchester County venues. Summer dance halls were popular in those days, as was the underground Pleasant Street Hall before The Lincolns moved to Legion Branch No. 26.

In fact, although Truro was the band's base, The Lincolns played their trademark R & B and soul around the Maritimes.

Until the band broke up in 1969, it was constantly in demand. Wherever they played, mostly at high school dances and college campuses, audiences were packed and appreciative. The band's main circuit was from Sydney to Yarmouth along one axis and from Dartmouth/Halifax up to Sackville, Moncton, Saint John, and Fredericton on another. Along the way, over a span of ten years, The Lincolns won thousands of fans with a songlist and intense performances that spoke to a generation.

Why and how, someone from a later era sometimes asks, was the Truro band so popular? And more than that: how come people are still talking about The Lincolns and still clamouring for reunions a half-century after they broke up?

I'm afraid I don't have a six-word sound bite answer. I'm going to need this whole book. But I do know that fun and intensity must be part of any formulation. In the pages that follow, based on interviews in late 2018 and early 2019 with band members and devoted followers, and on documentary and image research, I present the story of The Lincolns from the band's earliest days through its rise to prominence on to its dismemberment. It's a tale of growth and development, because nothing—including a rock 'n' roll band—emerges fully formed. There is always an evolution of some sort. In the case of The Lincolns, it was the evolution of a few somewhat goofy, aspiring kids in a small town into dynamic, committed musicians with a huge following across two provinces. It's a story with humour, joy, and sorrow, a history that takes readers backstage and on the road with the ever-travelling band. Inevitably, we also go out on the dance floor with diehard fans.

Along with telling The Lincolns's story, I also say something about the late 1950s and 1960s in the Maritimes, a time so very different from today. Hard as it might be to believe for those born after 1970 or so—who have always lived in a world with

Inglis Street, Truro, circa 1960; beyond is Exhibition Street, location of the Truro Legion.
(COURTESY OF THE COLCHESTER HISTOREUM)

seemingly endless subcategories of popular music, from grunge to punk and from psychedelic to electric powwow—back in that earlier era, rock 'n' roll was brand new. The genre's coming into being was like the Big Bang. Afterwards, there was this steadily expanding cosmos of popular music, an expansion that continues to this day.

Before that Big Bang, the songs that today are labelled "golden oldies" were absolutely fresh, never heard before. In fact, when rock 'n' roll first appeared in the mid-1950s, it was a heavy-beat style of music that many—adults, parents, teachers, church leaders—saw as frightening, even dangerous. This account appeared in a Vancouver newspaper in 1956 after a concert in the city by Bill Haley and His Comets:

This is the eight-man group who invented the craze that has barn-stormed its way across a continent in less than two years. Exactly what it is and how it weaves its hypnotic spell over addicted juveniles has never been accurately determined. But to the 4,630 delirious teen-agers who jived, stomped, kicked and shrieked their way through Haley's three-hour Wednesday night concert...the answers didn't matter.... The law surrendered the floor to the twitching, gyrating youngsters. The hall became a seething mass of flashing arms and legs, twisting torsos—loud with noise, sticky with heat. Faces were contorted, eyes glazed, mouths open. Mass hypnosis was in evidence. (Vancouver Sun, June 28, 1956)

Whether you think that's funny, quaint, or sad, the point is that, six decades ago, what now dominates the music industry was considered scary and its followers deranged. For a while in the 1950s, many radio stations, including CJCH in Halifax, banned Elvis Presley and other rockers from their airwaves. On the technology front, vinyl records had already come along. Less expensive and more durable than the brittle shellac 78s that preceded them, vinyl records meant that singles could be in many people's homes, as well as on jukeboxes in diners.

Music aside, many other aspects of life in the 1950s and early 1960s were also drastically different than today. One tiny example: my family's first Truro phone number was a mere four numbers, 2544. Another example: when my Grade 6 class visited the new Kelly Lake airport (today's Halifax Stanfield International) we could not get over that it had moving stairs! It was our first experience with an escalator.

The list of other differences is long, beginning with the absence of the internet and social media. No cellphones, video games, Netflix, or even cable TV. Until about the mid-fifties, few people in Nova Scotia even had a TV at all. When a family on my street got the first set, every kid hoped for an invitation to go watch *Howdy Doody* and *The Roy Rogers Show*. It wasn't long before other parents bought their own TV set: a big wooden box sitting in the living room. Initially, there was only one channel; then there were two. The networks that owned them broadcast only a few hours a day, leaving some of us staring at the Indian-head test pattern waiting for something to show up on the glowing screen.

What I'm describing must sound awful to later generations, who might feel sorry for we who lived in such unplugged-in times. Yet we felt no deprivation of things not yet invented. Besides, it's worth recalling that the 1960s witnessed incredible scientific and technological breakthroughs, with the United States and the Soviet Union racing for space and the moon. Back on Earth, in "the Hub of Nova Scotia," most of us under age twenty spent long hours face to face with other young people in highly public spaces, including parading up and down Truro's main drag, Prince Street. Most were on foot, but many were in cars, shooting the loop over and over again.

And then there were dances. Yes, dances. Dances were a really big thing, the absolute best way to observe, study, and connect with other young people. And if The Lincolns were playing, to revel in the powerhouse music generated by a charismatic band.

Please don't think I'm making the case that the 1950s and 1960s were some kind of lost utopia. Most definitely they were not. No period is without its problems, and the period I write about in this book certainly had its share of prejudices and negative stereotypes. Thankfully, there arose in the 1960s strong movements to overcome many of these handed-down ideas about religion, race, and gender.

To illustrate how things were in early 1960s Truro, when The Lincolns were just starting out, the first divide was between whether a person came from the East End or West End of town.

We actually believed that something of importance distinguished those who grew up on one side or the other of the railway tracks that more or less split Truro in half. My closest friends and I, growing up in the West End, attributed a mystique to East End girls. I'd like to think those East End girls felt the same about us.

After the East/West split, there were many other subdivisions. For instance, a union between a Protestant and a Catholic was then often called a "mixed marriage." When my sister's engagement to a Roman Catholic was announced, my mother's Protestant friends were aghast. "Can we stop it?" several asked in panicky phone calls. Someone heard speaking a language other than English—like French or Mi'kmaw—could bring stares or disapproving shakes of the head. I remember seeing and hearing people who spoke those other languages quickly switching to English.

As for matters relating to differing skin tones, Truro back then had three clearly demarcated areas where all Blacks lived: the Island, the Marsh, and the Hill. All three were on the margins of the town. It was not an official, institutionalized segregation as in the Jim Crow parts of the United States, but it was segregation nonetheless. Burnley "Rocky" Jones, born and raised in Truro, caused a stir when he called his home province Mississippi North, but he was speaking from his lived experience.

There was also a gulf between the Mi'kmaq and the non-Indigenous population. Back in the 1950s and early 1960s, the Millbrook First Nation—today a prosperous and forward-looking community—was then more commonly called Hollywood. It was a smug putdown, meant to be ironic because there were so many substandard dwellings on the reserve at that time.

As for questions of sexual orientation, "gay" was a word only poets used, to indicate they were happy. LGBTQ2, "gender fluidity," and "transitioning" were unknown terms, not to be invented for another generation or two. I recall that if in junior or senior high a guy came to school on a Thursday wearing something green it always prompted a snide remark: "You a fruit?" The imagined relationship between a particular colour and a particular day of the week was never explained. As a result of widespread prejudices, any who were drawn to members of their own sex kept it absolutely to themselves, to avoid mockery or abuse. Or worse. Yes, lives in Truro and elsewhere in Nova Scotia were lost over questions of sexual orientation. For at least one individual who played a leading role in the story of The Lincolns, the band offered a safe refuge away from the era's pressures and prejudices against homosexuals. That individual tells his own story in the Afterword of this book.

Of course, back in the 1960s, heterosexual relationships could also be fraught with worry and complications. Nothing like the #MeToo movement existed at the time, which meant that girls and women put up with many unwanted remarks and much unwanted touching. Career-wise, the message communicated to most girls fifty to sixty years ago was that there were but three choices: housewife, teacher, or nurse. Hard to believe, seeing as how, in the decades that followed, women would demonstrate that they could do absolutely everything.

As the sixties advanced, there seemed to be strife everywhere. In the United States, an inspiring civil rights movement and a contentious war in Vietnam took over the nightly news. Some young men from Truro and elsewhere in Nova Scotia served with the American forces in Vietnam, but most gladly kept their distance. In fact, the province welcomed thousands of draft dodgers. As the decade went on, it seemed like the majority of young people across the Western world—including in the Maritimes—were questioning pretty much everything. To underline just how different they felt from their parents, they grew their hair longer and many started wearing clothes no adult ever would—the girls wore skirts shorter than anyone alive had ever seen. Importantly, for females a certain pill came along that ushered in yet another revolution. It seemed to some, worried parents above all, as if the world and their kids were going crazy.

As a result, the period covered in this book can be seen alternately as simple or complicated. It was simple in terms of the available technologies, and complicated in the multiple revolutions taking place simultaneously in music and other popular-culture spheres.

In the midst of all the turmoil, thousands of young Nova Scotians and New Brunswickers flocked to the soul-stirring sounds of an R & B band out of Truro called The Lincolns. That group made eager crowds move and smile for the three or four hours they played. In the process, Lincolns dances became synonymous with releasing and expressing feelings, especially joy and exuberance. They were intense fun.

From the perspective of a half-century later, the musical era of the 1960s and its most engaging Maritime band might seem like a dream. But if so, to borrow the title of Otis Redding's classic song of vanished love, they are "Dreams to Remember." And if you never saw, heard, or danced to The Lincolns, well, that doesn't matter. The story that follows is still for you—if you're at all curious about a time before your own. This is a book about early rock 'n' roll, when a group of guys from a small Nova Scotia town set out to follow their dreams by playing the music they loved. Turn the page and come along for the ride.

IN THE BEGINNING
1957–61

Although we are talking about rock 'n' roll in mid-twentieth-century Nova Scotia, a 2,600-year-old Chinese proverb comes to mind. You know the one: *A journey of a thousand miles begins with a single step.*

For four young high school kids starting a band in central Nova Scotia in 1958, that first step must have seemed pretty tentative. None had a firm idea what further steps they should take or where they were going. All they knew for sure was that they liked rock 'n' roll and wanted to be part of it. That is, they didn't want just to listen and dance to the new music rapidly taking over youth culture; they wanted to make it themselves. If at all possible, before an audience.

First, however, they had to find kindred spirits. Then they would need practice, lots of practice, with at least the basic ingredients of a 1950s rock 'n' roll band: drums, guitars, maybe a piano or organ and a sax. Some combination of those were what one heard on the new records in jukeboxes and on nighttime radio, when Nova Scotians could listen to faraway American AM stations. To catch those broadcasts in Truro, kids with access to a car would drive up to the top of Wood Street, looking down on the town. Up there the reception was best. After dark, with their windows maybe steaming up—because people didn't *just* listen to the radio—they would tune in stations located in the Tri-Cities of upstate New York as well as WKBW in Buffalo and WINS in New York City. All those stations had deejays with big personalities who played songs by the likes of Bill Haley, Buddy Holly, Jerry Lee Lewis, The Everly Brothers, and Elvis.

Why did young people in Truro go to such trouble? Because it was fun. And exotic—dialling in to catch music coming over invisible airwaves from faraway. And because it was not always easy to hear that same music on Truro's own CKCL. There was a reason for that. Frank Cameron, later a well-known CHNS deejay and a CBC radio and TV personality, spun records at CKCL before moving to Halifax. Cameron recalled that, in 1958, the wife of the radio station's owner complained about hearing rock 'n' roll over the air in the evenings. Soon after, the station stopped playing that kind of music after dark. The stoppage, however, did not last. Cameron later began hosting a show broadcast live on CKCL that was a record hop for teens who came to the Truro Legion to dance on Friday nights. Hundreds attended, and hundreds more—maybe thousands—listened in.

The most prominent names on the American hit parade were generally white, mostly male. Because of a deep-seated racial divide, Black artists like Chuck Berry, Little Richard, and Big Mama Thornton received less play than they merited, except on the parallel but separate world of the R & B charts. Many mainstream American stations regarded R & B as "race music" and kept it off the air. That was both shameful and ironic. The irony was that rock 'n' roll had largely grown out of African American origins, just like blues and jazz. Yet the very Black artists who inspired many early white rock 'n' rollers did not get the same airplay as those who copied them. For instance, Big Mama Thornton's "Hound Dog" came out in 1952, four years before Elvis Presley's cover of the same song, yet it was only the latter's version that most white people ever heard. The most famous of the pale imitators was Pat Boone, who crooned "whitened" versions of various R & B songs by Black artists.

From time to time, mainstream American media did present glimpses of true rock 'n' roll artists to the broad public. The 1955 movie *Blackboard Jungle* famously opened and closed with the turbulent sound of Bill Haley's "Rock Around the Clock." Even better was a 1956 comedy starring Jayne Mansfield called *The Girl Can't Help It.* The soundtrack was filled with rock 'n' roll, and in numerous scenes viewers could see many of the acts performing in a Hollywood version of highly stylized nightclub settings. It's easy to imagine teens in Truro's Royal or Capitol theatre—and elsewhere in cinemas across Nova Scotia and around the Western world—being awestruck as they watched Little Richard, Fats Domino, Gene Vincent, The Platters, and others perform in Technicolor up on the big screen. How could the music-loving young not wish to enter such a world?

Though the big names in 1950s rock 'n' roll were overwhelmingly American, kids across the western hemisphere started dreaming of getting into the new genre. Across the Atlantic Ocean in Liverpool in 1957, fifteen-year-old Paul McCartney started playing with sixteen-year-old John Lennon. A year younger than McCartney were Mick Jagger and Keith Richards, who chanced to meet in a London train station in 1961 and discovered they both loved the same kind of music. And so began The Beatles and The Rolling Stones.

Tens of thousands of North American teenagers were doing precisely the same thing. In late 1950s Canada, there were two notable popular music success stories. Ottawa's Paul Anka

THE HIT PARADE, 1955–57

The top three songs of 1955 were "Cherry Pink and Apple Blossom White" by Perez Prado, "Rock Around the Clock" by Bill Haley and His Comets, and "The Yellow Rose of Texas" by Mitch Miller. "The Ballad of Davy Crockett" was released by two different artists; one came in at number six and the other at twenty-two.

A year later, the annual list was showing more rock 'n' roll. Elvis Presley had numbers one, two, eight, fourteen, and fifteen on the list for 1956. Bill Haley was at thirty-three with "See You Later Alligator," while Fats Domino with "Blueberry Hill" came in at forty-one. Little Richard's "Long Tall Sally" ended up at forty-five.

In 1957, rock 'n' roll was even more dominant. Elvis was back at number one with "All Shook Up," and he also had songs at nine, fourteen, and sixteen. Elsewhere on the list, Fats Domino had three songs, The Everly Brothers two, and Buddy Holly, Chuck Berry, and The Del-Vikings one each. With "Diana," Canada's Paul Anka was at number twenty-four, a few spots behind Sam Cooke at twenty with "You Send Me."

became a star when he wrote and sang hits like "Diana," "Lonely Boy," and "Put Your Head on My Shoulder." Also making the charts in the United States were four ex-choir boys from Toronto, singing as The Four Lads. A little later, beginning in 1960, Thunder Bay's Bobby Curtola came up with songs that would be well known across Canada and sometimes charted in the States.

In Truro, by 1957 one band already had a local following. That was The Novatones, a bunch of guys in their late teens. The players varied from time to time, but the group began in Bill MacNeil's basement, with Bill on drums, Wayne Mills on guitar, and Layne Francis on sax. Later, Anthony (Sonny) Johnson sometimes played rhythm guitar. At first, they tackled already classic songs such as "Rock Around the Clock" and "Slippin' and Slidin'." Adding James Paris as singer, they called themselves The Novatones. "Screamin' J," as Paris styled himself, had a good voice. More important, he was able to channel some of the spirit of the ultimate mid-1950s rock 'n' roll superstar, Little Richard.

(As a footnote, in the early 1980s Truro's Screamin' J Paris would be the inspiration for the ghost-like Screamin' John McGee in John MacLachlan Gray's hit musical, *Rock and Roll*. Gray had never seen the real Paris perform, but he had heard enough about him growing up in Truro to create a theatrical character inspired by those accounts.)

Whenever and wherever The Novatones played, Truro's young fans of rock 'n' roll came to listen. In part, that's because it wasn't easy in Nova Scotia to hear the new music on local radio. But it was also because The Novatones were good musicians. They sounded great, and by their example they inspired an entire generation of younger people to try their hand. Photos taken during a 1957 show featuring some of The Novatones at Truro's Capitol Theatre (normally a place for movies) reveal a small portion of what was a large and raucous crowd of youngsters.

A Novatones concert in the Capitol Theatre, Truro, 1957; visible are three individuals who would be important in the story of The Lincolns: onstage, playing sax, is Layne Francis; down in the front-row seats, are future Lincolns pianist Peter Harris (circled on the left) and bass guitarist Brian Chisholm (circled on the right).
(COURTESY OF LAYNE FRANCIS)

It didn't take long for some to be up jiving in the aisles. Two who would help shape the early history of The Lincolns, Peter Harris and Brian Chisholm, were there that day, right in the front row.

The racial divide in Nova Scotia during those days is most famously illustrated by the 1946 incident involving Viola Desmond at New Glasgow's Roseland Theatre, when she was put in jail for sitting downstairs and not up in the balcony reserved for Blacks. For standing up for her civil rights, Desmond posthumously received many honours, including replacing Canada's first prime minister, Sir John A. Macdonald, on the country's ten dollar bill. In Truro, too, Blacks were expected to sit up in the balcony in the town's cinemas. Current Truro town councillor Danny Joseph remembers as a kid noticing how Black friends automatically headed upstairs while he proceeded to the ground floor seating area.

He thought it was simply where they preferred to sit. Not until years later did he fully understand.

Back in that era, there were unwritten restrictions on the kind of jobs people of African descent were able to apply for in Truro and which shops they were welcomed in, including for haircuts. There were even separate washrooms in some schools. Was racial separation enforced at concerts in the Capitol Theatre? It seems unlikely, since Screamin' J, the lead singer of The Novatones, was Black. But then racism doesn't have anything to do with what is *likely*. It's about prejudices handed down from earlier times.

The Novatones's music was basically their versions of songs on the hit parade. Today, we call them *covers*, but I don't recall ever hearing that term back in the 1960s. They were just songs, immensely popular songs. Everyone starting out playing tunes by others, including the big-name British groups. The Beatles had hits of their own with tunes previously recorded by other artists, such as "Please Mr. Postman" and "Twist and Shout." Recording even more covers were the early Rolling Stones. Most of their first album features songs previously released by Black American R & B singers. As for Truro's Novatones, they did release one record of their own, with "Mary Lee" on one side and "Please Come Back" on the other. Sitting in for the Halifax recording session were Austin Bigsby on drums and Waldo Munro on piano, the latter best known as the piano player on the hit TV show *Don Messer's Jubilee*. Frank Cameron, then a Truro deejay, had a hand in the lyrics of those two original Novatones songs, while Wayne Mills and Layne Francis wrote the music. That same Layne Francis would later join The Lincolns, but I am getting ahead of the story I have in mind.

That story begins with a set of drums, a gift from a mother to her teenage son.

During the late 1940s and throughout the 1950s, Mrs. Margaret Norrie, a widow and former professor of biology at Mount Allison University, raised four kids on a farm outside Truro. Mrs. Norrie made sure each child was introduced to music of a classical nature, and each was made to take violin or piano lessons. Roderick, the youngest, born in 1942 and often called Roddie, disliked the violin classes he was compelled to take. He felt even more strongly about festival performances. "I hated it," Rod Norrie recalled more than sixty years later. "It was just scales and posture three days a week. Hold your head and neck like this. It was awful."

Rod also has a painful memory of singing onstage while in elementary school in Truro. "I was scared to death. It was chorus and solo, sight reading, then singing solo and chorus." One Christmas concert at Alice Street School he had to sing a solo with a costume that included a large star surrounding his face. When it was over, the teacher responsible for keeping the show moving stripped Rod of his costume "in front of all the girls in my class. They all laughed, and I died a thousand deaths." The experience made Rod never want to sing in public again.

After three years of trying to get Rod to play the violin, Mrs. Norrie gave up—on *that* instrument. She did not, however, give up on music for her youngest child. In the aftermath of the Second World War, there were often parades on Truro streets by the military or by Scottish associations, both of which featured pipes and drums. Mrs. Norrie noticed how attentive Rod always was to the drummers when they marched past. He absolutely studied them. Something clicked in Mrs. Norrie's head, and one day in 1958, when Rod was sixteen, she came back from a trip to Toronto with a set of drums—white drums. No other kids in Truro had their own set of drums at the time. Rod was more than surprised; he was delighted. He began to fool around to see what he could do with the

His mother's gift of a drum set was a turning point in Rod Norrie's appreciation for music—and in his life.

(COURTESY OF ROD AND ELEANOR NORRIE)

sticks but found it not much fun to play alone, with no other musicians or instruments. He longed to play music like he heard on the Little Richard records he owned. He played those, especially "Long Tall Sally," over and over again until the disc literally wore out.

We'll come back to Rod Norrie's drum set in a moment, but first let's turn to the guitar, the most conspicuous of rock 'n' roll instruments of the 1950s and early 1960s. At the time, many instrumentals featuring guitars topped the charts, ranging from the twangy sound of Duane Eddy to the pulsating tunes of The Ventures. Eddy is said to have sold twelve million records by 1963, while The Ventures' interpretation of "Walk, Don't Run" was a massive worldwide hit. Out of England came The Shadows, another band that sold millions of records as both the backup band for Cliff Richard and as instrumentalists on their own.

I have no idea how many teenagers in the Truro area started playing guitars in 1958, but there were more than a few. Each hoped to capture the essence of the new rock 'n' roll. One of those kids was Frank Mumford, who was born in Halifax in 1943 but grew up in the Onslow area, outside Truro. There's a story

Frank Mumford (1943–2004), a naturally gifted guitarist, became a hero to younger players.
(COURTESY OF HEATHER MUMFORD)

behind how and why Frank got that first guitar. It's a story that speaks of a childhood illness and a father's love.

When Frank Mumford was twelve years old, he suffered from Osgood-Schlatter disease, a condition that strikes some children and adolescents during growth spurts. The bones and cartilage grow much faster than the muscles and tendons. The result is severe pain during physical activity. In Frank's case, the doctors put casts on both legs and left them on for about six months. Frank's father was a truck driver who drove around the Maritimes. On one of those trips, early on in Frank's illness, Mr. Mumford picked up a guitar. He himself was a long-time fiddler, and he hoped his son might be interested in learning an instrument. The guitar wasn't fancy or expensive, just a simple acoustic model. But for twelve-year-old Frank, it was a start.

With nothing much else to do because of the casts on his legs, Frank played his father's gift every chance he got. With natural talent and eager determination, he quickly became proficient. From the vantage point of middle age, Frank recounted what happened next. "I hadn't been playing the guitar long when some guys in the neighbourhood heard that I was pretty good and had a different style, which was a rhythm and blues style. There was a knock on the door and—just like that—I was invited to a jam session." Whether it was all the practice, or some innate genetic gift, Frank Mumford developed a great ear for music. In his head he could tell the key to every song he heard. That talent would be invaluable to The Lincolns in the years ahead.

Meanwhile, in the town of Truro, right beside the junior high, Brian Chisholm (born in 1943) was being raised by a loving single mother, Sally Campbell Chisholm (later Bates). While Brian was still a toddler, Sally's husband had scampered off to Louisiana and never returned, leaving her responsible for bringing up her son. Sally made a modest income working in the ladies' department at Margolians, a renowned Truro store that sold clothes and footwear. Brian, an only child, was the absolute centre of Sally's world. She could see how smart and musical her boy was, and what a charmer he could be. To make him happy, Sally ordered a guitar from the Simpsons catalogue. Brian was more than pleased. Overnight, guitar strap around his neck, the free-spirited, outspoken, mischievous teenager began to picture himself as a rock 'n' roller just like Gene Vincent or Buddy Holly. Now that he had his own guitar, he began to dream that one day he too would play rock 'n' roll up on a stage somewhere.

Elsewhere in Truro—specifically in a bungalow at 50 Whitman Court—Peter Harris (born in 1943) was growing up in a family that owned a prominent shoe store on Prince Street. Unlike Frank Mumford and Brian Chisholm, Peter Harris *did*

The Lincolns's Brian Chisholm as a young man.
(COURTESY OF SHARON MACKAY)

have formal music training. In fact, by 1958 he had studied piano for eight years. His parents loved music and encouraged their two sons to learn different instruments. Along the way, teenaged Peter was drawn to playing rock 'n' roll tunes by ear, just as he'd seen Fats Domino, Little Richard, and Jerry Lee Lewis do on TV. And the more into his teenage years Peter advanced, the more he preferred the new music over the classical repertoire he had learned as a lad. I can imagine the ear-to-ear grin on his face the first time he heard Chuck Berry's 1956 hit single "Roll Over Beethoven." It was a song that celebrated the new music over the old—Berry taunting Beethoven to tell Tchaikovsky the news.

Besides his proficiency on the piano, Peter Harris possessed another important asset: a virtually empty basement in his parents' home. It was not the slightest bit finished or furnished. There was no carpet or panelling, nor any furniture—nothing but concrete, and used only for storage. But there was enough space for Peter's piano. Down there, the sound of his pounding out rock 'n' roll at least would be muffled for his parents. They loved him dearly but were adamant that he concentrate on his education; although not forbidding him to play the noisy new stuff, they did their best to discourage it.

So, with his love of rock 'n' roll and a basement to practise in, Peter Harris's next challenge was to find a few like-minded souls to see what they could do with their different instruments.

In the summer of 1958, Peter Harris, Frank Mumford, and Brian Chisholm decided to form a band with their piano and two guitars. Frank was the better guitarist, so he played lead while Brian played rhythm guitar. But they absolutely needed someone to play drums. A friend, George Boyce, piped up that Rod Norrie had a brand new drum set, likely the only one in town owned by a kid their age. Peter, Frank, and Brian all knew and liked Rod, so they urged George to see if Rod would loan him his new kit.

Out to the Norrie farm went George Boyce one Saturday to ask his school friend Rod if he could borrow his Toronto-bought drums. He explained that he wanted them for a rock 'n' roll session at Peter Harris's place. Rod knew Peter and Brian from Colchester County Academy (CCA, later Truro Senior High), and Frank from literally crossing paths with him along a country road near his house. But if Rod secretly wished he was the one getting a chance to play his drum kit with those three guys, he didn't let that sentiment get in the way. Big-hearted Rod Norrie said yes: George Boyce could borrow his drums as long as he brought them back undamaged.

The next day Rod looked out the window of the family home and saw a car in the driveway. It wasn't George. It was Frank

Mumford, Brian Chisholm, and Peter Harris. They had Rod's drum set in the trunk.

"George can't play the goddamn drums," they said. "Can you play, Rod?"

Rod thought about how often he'd watched the drummer of The Novatones and then tried to duplicate the sounds on his own set. He said: "I can get by, but not do anything cute." He added: "No promises, but I'll do my best."

"Okay," said Mumford, Harris, and Chisholm. "We're having a get-together next Saturday down in Peter's basement. Will you bring your drums?"

"I will. Hey, thanks."

And that was how what would become The Lincolns began— the name was not yet on anyone's lips—in a basement on Truro's Whitman Court. Rod could indeed play the drums, though only the basics back then. He'd substituted one night at the stadium in New Glasgow for The Novatones when their drummer couldn't make it. Rod recalled: "I got through it, but just barely." With that experience, and knowing how to keep the beat and play with drive—laying the foundation for the other instruments—Rod was what Harris, Mumford, and Chisholm were looking for: their drummer.

Together, the four young guys learned songs that matched their tastes and talents at the time. That meant mostly instrumentals in the beginning. Rod Norrie recalled being so impressed by Frank Mumford's guitar playing on "Johnny Be Good" that he called his girlfriend, Eleanor Tucker, on the phone so she could listen in, which she patiently did for several minutes. Over time, the boys tackled songs with lyrics, like "Bony Moronie," "Long Tall Sally," and "Alley Oop." In the process of making music, the four became fast friends. With no up-front dedicated singer, the two guitarists and the pianist chimed in on the vocals.

What did it feel like finally to be doing what they'd imagined? It's not easy to put into words, but in *Petty: The Biography* author Warren Zanes quotes Tom Petty (1950–2017) as expressing the feeling this way: "'The first time you count four and, suddenly, rock and roll is playing—it's bigger than life itself.... It was the greatest moment in my experience, really. I couldn't believe it was happening, that we were making music. No one can understand what a blast to the moon that is unless they've done it.'" My guess is that Petty's description pretty much describes how Rod, Frank, Brian, and Peter felt down in the Harris's basement.

If the four players were now a band, they needed a name. Frank Mumford recalled they "were interested in priority stuff, like beer, cars, and girls...but since we didn't want to name the band Moosehead or...after one of our girlfriends, we picked a car we all thought was pretty neat." The selection was a brand new vehicle, the Valiant, released by Plymouth in the fall of 1959 for the 1960 model year. The four young men became The Valiants.

So named, the young men continued to practise in Peter Harris's basement, and sometimes at friend Tom Stanfield's house, where there was a piano, or out at Mrs. Norrie's on her baby grand. Eventually, they felt they were ready to play in public.

Their first gig was at an Allied Youth Club dance at Truro Junior High, for which the boys were paid, collectively, $30. Sounds like a pittance, but that's about $255 in today's purchasing power—so, not bad for four high school kids. "It was just great," said Rod in 2018. The band sought other engagements and soon played in nearby Onslow and Stewiacke. At the latter venue, Peter Harris startled the other three guys with his pre-show preparations. Before the crowd was allowed in, Peter kept moving the school's piano around the stage, trying to figure out where it should go. He liked to play like Little Richard and Jerry Lee Lewis, pounding the keys while looking at and singing to

CARS WERE US

In the late 1950s and early 1960s, cars were everything. They were as big as boats, and gas was so cheap that today it's hard to believe—roughly the equivalent of ten cents a litre. Back then, nobody gave the environment much thought, so they burned gas in guzzling cars for the fun of it. And the speed of it. Young people in the Truro I grew up in—well, typically boys more than girls—knew the cubic inches and horsepower of every engine in every car, and how fast the fastest ones went when they showed up at a drag strip. Or whose car had just beat someone else's car on the straight stretch of highway near the Starway Drive-In on the outskirts of Bible Hill. It was known as "the Norrie stretch" because it passed by the family home of The Valiants' drummer. It was a popular drag zone—complete with teenaged flagmen—where cars raced side by side down the road, ignoring the illegality and great risk of it all. It was, as the saying goes, a different era. To show just how car-oriented that period was, I recall a summer day standing with a friend at the corner of Willow and Roosevelt Streets writing down the licence plate numbers of every car that went by. When we spied plates from another province or state, we actually thought we had accomplished something special. Crazy, eh?

the audience. On this day in Stewiacke, Peter moved the piano once too often. A little too enthusiastically, over-eager Peter accidently shoved the upright piano right off the stage. Down to the floor it crashed. The entire band was startled, then roared with laughter. Together, they helped Peter get the damaged piano back up onstage.

More lucrative for The Valiants than playing schools were the summertime dance halls. They played in three regularly: at Brule, Shortts Lake, and Truro's East Prince Street. The owner of the three halls charged the band $50 (about $420 today) to rent each one. The band then had to hire the police and get friends, most often girlfriends, to look after the gate (hundreds of coins to collect, count, and divvy up)—in other words, they and their friends had to do all of the work! The good news was that a few hundred people would show up at these summer dance halls, keen to move to the sounds of live rock 'n' roll. These were where everybody came to meet their friends and to demonstrate out on the dance floor how well they could already dance or else learn how.

Word of mouth about The Valiants was positive, and the crowds got steadily bigger each week. As well, the band sometimes hired a sound car owned by Esso dealer T. Weldon Mills to get the word out. A sound car was a vehicle with cone-shaped loudspeakers on top, which went around town announcing the time and place of the next dance. In an era when no one wore ear buds or stared at a cellphone, it was an effective means of publicity.

The main dance then was jiving, but in the late 1950s some teens loved to do "The Stroll" as well. This was a dance craze where baggy-panted boys and long-skirted girls formed two separate lines, a wide aisle between them. The first boy and girl in each line would meet in the middle, join hands, and slowly stroll away, weaving their steps down the aisle. That first couple then would separate and rejoin their respective lines and wait for all the other pairs, one by one, to do the same thing.

The Valiants appreciated having money in their pockets from the dances, but they needed more than what came in through occasional gigs. They had instruments and amps to buy and repair, and no local stores would rent to young musicians. Long & McQuade came into existence in 1956 but was not in Nova Scotia until later. So Mrs. Norrie often gave the boys loans, which the lads always paid back fully—in nickels, dimes, and quarters after each dance. Mrs. Norrie was more than pleased to help them out, and pleased again to see them accept their responsibility to repay their debts.

Besides practising and performing, The Valiants kept tabs on The Novatones. "Wherever they played," Rod Norrie recalled in 2018, "that's where we'd go." In 1958, Rod and Eleanor Tucker and two other couples even followed The Novatones over to Charlottetown, Prince Edward Island, where the Truro group appeared on a live TV broadcast. The teens headed off to catch the ferry from Cape Tormentine, New Brunswick. When they arrived at the Charlottetown motel they had booked, they were astonished to be greeted in the lobby by Mrs. Norrie and Mrs. Tucker. The two mothers were not taking any chances: they had hurried across to the Island on the ferry from Caribou. The next day, Rod and Eleanor and other couples danced on TV, *American Bandstand*-style, in front of The Novatones and other musicians. To the Truro-area sixteen-year-olds, jiving and strolling to rock 'n' roll on television—the new music on the new technology—was "a big deal."

Rod Norrie remembered that the guys in The Novatones were generous to the younger musicians in town, including his Valiants. Novatones guitarist Wayne Mills passed playing tips on to Frank Mumford and even loaned him a better guitar than

COURTING 1957-STYLE

The first date Eleanor Tucker and Rod Norrie went on was anything but ordinary. It was 1957, and they were both fifteen and in Grade 10 at Colchester County Academy. Rod asked Eleanor to go with him to a movie at the drive-in theatre in Hilden, and she said yes. But there was one complication: Rod had no driver's licence. Not to worry. Rod had driven his mother's car occasionally on country roads since he was thirteen. How much harder could it be to drive to Hilden, a mere twenty kilometres away? So, Rod borrowed the keys to his mother's two-toned green 1956 Oldsmobile. You could call it theft, but borrowing has a nicer ring. In 2018, I asked Rod and Eleanor what was on the screen, but neither could recall. "It wasn't really the movie we were going to see," explained Eleanor. After the show, Rod drove her home, only to have the police pull up behind the Oldsmobile in front of her King Street house. While Rod talked to the cops through his rolled-down window, Eleanor fled from the car, up the steps, and into her house. "Like, zoom," said Rod. "He has never forgiven me," Eleanor explained. The police gave Rod a warning but laid no charges. In the years to come, Rod would become friends with many police officers who were assigned to cover Lincolns dances.

the one Frank owned. Twenty years later, at a Lincolns Reunion in 1978, the same Wayne Mills brought his grandson to see The Lincolns play at the Nova Scotia Teachers College. Rod Norrie told the grandson that night that his grandfather had taught each of these Lincolns how to play rock 'n' roll—an exaggeration, but of the good kind. Wayne Mills and his grandson both beamed with pride. After that, any time there was a gathering of musicians, Wayne Mills would always come looking for Rod to say hello. It's a recollection Rod treasures to this day.

In August 1959, seventeen-year-old Rod Norrie went off on a short motor trip to Maine with Truro friend Gary Blaikie. Rod was at the wheel of his mother's 1958 black and white Chevrolet near Auburn, Maine, when an oncoming car suddenly crossed onto Rod's side, blindly passing four cars. There was a head-on collision. When the crumpled Chevy settled, Rod knew his right leg was broken. He was relieved to see that Gary Blaikie and the hitchhiker they'd picked up were only dazed, not injured. The driver who had caused the accident walked up to Rod and said through the wreckage, "I'm sorry." Rod crawled out of the Chevrolet by pulling himself through a tight opening at the top of his peeled-back driver's door. He was taken to a hospital in Bangor, where his leg was set and a cast applied. When the hospital called Rod's mother back in Nova Scotia, she fainted. Her eldest daughter, Margie, took the phone. Rod was two weeks in the hospital before he came back home. He would not be able to walk on that leg for nearly a year.

Throughout the rest of 1959 and into 1960, while Rod Norrie's right leg was healing inside a cast, the young drummer had to adjust how to play his instrument, switching to his left foot to beat the bass drum. That's unusual for drummers: generally, they have a single dominant side, either right or left, depending on which hand they mostly use. Because of the accident,

Rod Norrie's damaged Chevrolet, Maine, 1959.
(COURTESY OF ROD AND ELEANOR NORRIE)

Rod now became a right-handed, left-footed drummer—and that's how he stayed even after the cast came off in 1960.

As the weeks ticked by, Frank, Peter, Brian, and Rod got steadily better as musicians and tighter in their sound. As 1960 rolled on, The Valiants began to think they had made a mistake with their name. The car they'd chosen was altogether too or-dinary—a modest family car. A rock 'n' roll band, they now felt, should be called something more striking and classy. A later era of rock 'n' rollers might have come up with a wry or sarcastic name—"The Traffic Jams" or "The Beat-Up Buicks"—but this was still 1960. Instead, the Truro band, still enamoured with automobiles, zeroed in on a luxury car made by Mercury and rebranded themselves as The Lincolns. The name, it would turn out, would have great appeal and a long life in Nova Scotia, with a degree of brand recognition a half-century after the band officially broke up.

Some say "The Lincolns" was chosen during a practice session at Rod Norrie's mother's place in Onslow. Winston (Dink) MacDonald, a friend of the guys in the band, happened to be there and he recalled that Rod and Layne Francis were the ones who championed the name. Winston said it was the Sunday of the 1960 Labour Day weekend. He could date it because the next day he was heading to New Glasgow to get ready to begin his first teaching job.

Yet the band's new name first appeared in print in the 1960 edition of the *Critic*, the CCA yearbook, which came out in May or June. In it, each student graduating from Grade 12 was allowed a paragraph, and in the write-up on Peter Harris the second sentence read: "His chief interest outside school is the Rock 'n Roll band The Lincolns." It seems that Peter was talking about The Lincolns before anyone else. Despite his high school yearbook entry, however, Peter Harris did not remain a Lincoln for long, but exactly when he left the band is lost in the mists of time and faded memory. Sixty years later, the thinking is that it corresponded with his going off to Dalhousie University in the fall of 1960. Rod Norrie went to Mount Allison that same fall but tried to get back to Truro every weekend to make music with his buddies. Peter Harris's life went in a different direction.

Around the time Peter Harris drifted away from The Lincolns, or maybe a little earlier, Truro's top band, the slightly older Novatones, broke up when Screamin' J Paris moved to Montreal to advance his singing career. He would do well there, joining a band called The Vikings; eventually, Paris would move back to Truro and sing in a local church choir. The Novatones's sometime drummer and singer Ritchie Moss went on to become an arm-wrestling champ under the name of Clayton Moss. The Novatones's breakup made it possible for Layne Francis, the band's self-taught and highly regarded sax player, to join another

Layne Francis became Truro's top sax player while still in his teens, and loved to play jazz, blues, and rock 'n' roll.
(COURTESY OF LAYNE FRANCIS)

group. First that was The Blue Cats, based in New Glasgow, whose singer was Harold Borden. Then, Francis was invited to become a member of Truro's newly named The Lincolns.

Layne Francis was born in Truro in 1940 and grew up on the town's most prestigious street, Smith Avenue. His father initially owned a grocery store in town, then a hobby store. Layne recalls that, growing up, he had long wanted to play the trumpet, clarinet, or saxophone but didn't have one. Then, in 1955, when Layne was fifteen, his father gave him forty dollars to buy a used sax: a 1928 Conn satin silver C melody model, with its original pads but no case. Pitched to the key of C, it was midway in size between a tenor and an alto sax. Layne taught himself to play it, which meant that, in the beginning, there were some screechy days and nights. In 2018 he recalled that he "locked the instrument nightly in my bedroom for two months and drove the neighbours crazy" while he "figured out how it works." Former neighbour Brian MacIntosh agreed: he remembered hearing all kinds of "crazy noises" coming out through Layne's bedroom window as he learned how to play.

Layne grew up listening to the music of the 1940s and early 1950s and especially liked Louis Armstrong, Count Basie, and Glenn Miller. When rock 'n' roll burst onto the scene in the mid-1950s, he fell for it like everyone else his age, though he retained an affection for jazz as well. Layne Francis would have been a terrific addition to any band, since he had such a depth of musical knowledge, which he was always willing to share. And his mellow sax meant that whatever group he was with could tackle a wider range of songs than just those with guitars and drums. Layne didn't just play the sax, he played it like the notes were sweet as honey, and when he became a member of The Lincolns, it was a major step forward for the band.

Aside from his abundant musical talents, Layne Francis had another great asset: he owned a car. For the next several years, it would usually fall to Layne and Rod Norrie to drive The Lincolns and their equipment to all their gigs.

It is worth pausing for a moment to reflect on how all these young musicians who made up the original Lincolns got to this point in the story. Each had help from a parent to obtain his instruments, and some received encouragement as well, but aside from that, each of their individual journeys into rock 'n' roll was driven by some internal desire. My guess is that it was much the same for teenagers everywhere across the Western world in the 1950s. Few parents led the way, signing their kids up for lessons to play the new music in the hope they would one day become another Little Richard or Elvis Presley. God forbid! They wanted their teenagers to become lawyers or accountants or to work as mechanics or clerks in a store—something that was predictable and would bring in a regular paycheque. To venture into rock 'n' roll was an exclusive teenage dream, not that of any parent at the time.

I tend to think that, with their new rock 'n' roll identity, the four guys in The Lincolns in late 1960—Brian Chisholm, Frank Mumford, Rod Norrie, and Layne Francis—walked around their hometown a little taller than before. How could they not, especially among people their own age? After all, regardless of how good or bad they were at algebra or biology, or how talented they were at sports, they were members of an actual band. And a popular one at that. They were no longer Valiants but Lincolns! Gone were the days when they were simply a clutch of guys practising in basements and bedrooms. They were playing before responsive, dancing crowds. It was a great feeling. "It feels good," Layne Francis—a man of few words—once told an interviewer. "The band feels good."

Excitement, satisfaction, and accomplishment were feelings each and every Lincoln shared. Those feelings were strongest during live performances, but in the early days they were also present when the band members walked past or went into George's, the go-to restaurant on Truro's Prince Street in the early 1960s. George's was the local mecca for older teens and young adults. A factor in its popularity was that it was only about fifty steps from the Pleasant Street Hall, where the renown of The Lincolns began to climb. When the band played there in the early 1960s, the venue was known to most simply as Hopgoods, because Hopgoods was the name of the IGA grocery store at ground level. But the hall had several other names as well. A

WHERE THE COOL KIDS HANG

Every town has at least one—a place where the cool kids, or those aspiring to be, hang out. In Truro in the late 1950s and early 1960s, that place was George's, named after its owner, George MacCharles. With booths and counter stools, George's was where high school students, college kids, and young working adults went to be seen. (If you were in junior high, you had better beat it farther down Prince Street to Layton's, another popular hangout.) In George's, the girls sipped cherry Cokes and shared chips with gravy (or enjoyed cake donuts topped with ice cream) while the boys tried to act and look like movie heartthrob James Dean. Whether they had brushcuts or ducktails, the guys would tease and show off. Outside, holding up the building night after night, were what singer Frank MacKay came to call the "perpetuals." They numbered eight to ten, all guys, talking cars or teasing girls when they went by.

few called it the IGA-à-Go-Go, perhaps because in the early years The Lincolns hired some go-go girls to come up from Halifax to dance. Why from Halifax, when Truro had lots of girls who could dance? Well, the girls in question were regular dancers on the TV show out of Halifax called *Frank's Bandstand*.

Another name for the Pleasant Street Hall was "the pit." That was understandable, since the hall was underground, down a single set of stairs that, for the public, was the only way in or out. (If fire regulations required a second exit, they were not observed.) The hall was a former bowling alley that had become a bingo hall. Its ceiling was pretty low, which is maybe why the walls were painted white and pale blue, with red balloons rising up, in an attempt to make the ceiling appear higher than it really was. The balloon motif artwork was painted by the building's owner, Abie Salem, who gave the space the name "Danceland."

When The Lincolns first played the hall, the stage was in an area with washrooms overhead on the floor above. One night during a dance, a plumbing mishap occurred, with water cascading through the floor onto drummer Rod Norrie's head. After that, the stage was moved to a roped-in area at the other end of the hall. Despite its subterranean location, the space was far from dungeon-like. Besides, when The Lincolns were playing there, it hardly mattered. The relatively small dance floor was crowded, which made the place feel something like a nightclub, minus tables, chairs, or any kind of liquor licence. Pop and chips were all the canteen carried, and intermissions would often send attendees outside, over to George's for refreshment. Nonetheless, Danny Joseph thought the place had a "secretive, speakeasy" atmosphere. But then, Danny was only twelve or thirteen at the time.

As long as the live music kept coming, the Pleasant Street Hall was jumping. Doreen Woodworth (née Cameron) remembered getting drives over from Tatamagouche so she and five or six girlfriends could attend Lincolns dances. In Doreen's words, "We loved the band and it was a fun place to go." Jud Pearson recalled "everyone singing along (we all knew the words) and everyone having big smiles on their faces, having a great time." With a broad grin, Gay Pearson added: "It was fun; it was so much fun."

At this stage of their career, The Lincolns had no full-time singer. Layne Francis remembers that, back then, "we mostly played instrumentals." He singled out "Rudy's Rock," a Bill Haley tune released in 1956, and "Red River Rock," released by Johnny and The Hurricanes in 1959, both of which featured a prominent sax solo. When there were songs with lyrics, Brian Chisholm apparently did most of the singing while playing bass, with lead guitarist Frank Mumford chiming in. Renowned playwright and novelist John MacLachlan Gray, who would later join The Lincolns for two years, recalled going to see the band play while he was in junior high. What he remembered was a group that "relied a whole lot on instrumentals featuring Layne on sax." And while Brian "wasn't much of a singer," he had "lots of charisma."

Indeed, Brian Chisholm had charisma in spades. He was a natural showman, someone who loved to perform for an audience. Karen MacLean, a girlfriend of Frank Mumford, said of Brian that "no sweeter guy ever lived." He was also the epitome of a free spirit. Brian had a mind that was totally his own, and he wouldn't do or wear anything he didn't think was cool. He also never missed a chance to engage with fans standing near the stage, especially females. And for their part, the people at the dances had a hard time taking their eyes off him. In Brian Chisholm's 2011 obituary, specific mention was made of two songs he was especially "remembered for": "Keep A-Knockin'" and "Roll Over Beethoven."

Already, Frank Mumford was showing at rehearsals and dances just how important he was to the group: his ear was that good. As Rod Norrie put it in late 2018, "Frank Mumford was the go-to guy if anyone had a question about the music we were playing. He was pretty much the boss." And that's what the lead guitarist would remain—a virtual conductor—throughout the band's entire lifespan. (When at the 2018 Lincolns Reunion someone commented to Barry Ryan that the songs sometimes went on a little long, Barry replied: "That's because Frank Mumford's not here anymore to say 'Enough!' And then signal to the band that it was time to wrap it up.")

In these early days, individuals, male and female, occasionally would ask for a tryout with The Lincolns. Some played an instrument and some sang, and some were more talented than others. None was exactly what the four guys in the band were hoping for, which was someone with a strong voice who could sing rock 'n' roll. Two older guys—men in their twenties—started coming around and acting as if they were part of the band, though no one had asked them to join. It's likely best not to reveal their names, but one had been an occasional drummer with The Novatones and could entertain a crowd with a few jokes and songs; the other had a genuinely good singing voice.

On the surface, perhaps, maybe some thought the two newcomers were making The Lincolns better. Frank, Rod, Brian, and Layne did not agree. They resented that somehow these older newcomers were acting as if The Lincolns was their band, and they were always bossing the younger guys around. Still ticked off nearly sixty years later, Rod Norrie describes the duo as "bullies. They were brutes. A-holes. They wanted to run us and gave us hell all the time. They were bad news." One day, loud words were exchanged, with the duo demanding space be made for them in a crowded car by having the girls inside get out. Through an open car window, Eleanor Tucker, Rod Norrie's girlfriend, blurted out: "They don't need you two anyway." That would prove to be true, but at the time it took a lot of nerve to say it out loud. (It was an advance peek at the gumption Eleanor Norrie would show decades later when she became a Member of Nova Scotia's Legislative Assembly and a government minister.)

The misgivings and hard feelings about the two self-appointed occasional frontmen went on for a few months, until one evening in September 1961. That night, while The Lincolns were performing at the Pleasant Street Hall without the bad news duo anywhere in sight, the solution showed up. A young, pleasant-faced, nervously smiling, slightly chubby guy came up to the stage, as others had done before, and asked politely if he could sing a song or two as a tryout. At least one of the guys in the band knew exactly who he was—a Grade 10 student at CCA who happened to have a powerful singing voice—but the other Lincolns did not know the seventeen-year-old.

It didn't take long for everyone in the band—through knowing nods and smiles—to grasp that this new singer at the microphone was not like any other singer they'd heard before. Frank MacKay—for that was the young man's name—owned the Little Richard song he was asked to sing. The audition changed The Lincolns. As Rod Norrie recalled in late 2018, fifty-seven years after that night, "The sky lit up and Gabriel blew his horn. There is a God and his name is Frank MacKay. We all remember that time and what a pleasure it was. We took a huge step forward that day. Happiness is a great singer—we all agree. This was the moment that made The Lincolns."

READY TO ROLL... AND ROCK
1961–64

*S*eventeen-year-old Frank MacKay had not shown up at the Pleasant Street Hall that evening in September 1961 because a line in his horoscope said he should take a chance—not at all. A few days earlier, during the first week of school, The Lincolns's bass player, Brian Chisholm, had sauntered up to him in the hallway of the CCA. As Frank remembers it, Brian, who was in Grade 12, wondered if he, Frank, a new kid in Grade 10, would be interested in having a tryout as the singer with The Lincolns. Brian likely had heard Frank sing somewhere, and knew talent when he heard it. Acting on behalf of the band, but without telling them, Brian thought this kid might be the answer to their current problem: two bullying older singers whom no one in The Lincolns liked.

The place where Brian Chisholm likely heard Frank MacKay sing was at the Truro Legion. Frank performed there one night with another local band, The Corvettes, a short-lived group featuring David Gass, Gary Pye, Doug Moore, Tom Rogerson, and Lee Taylor—the very same Lee Taylor who in 1962 would join The Lincolns as second saxophone. Or maybe Brian had simply heard talk about the young singer from others who had heard him perform. Either way, he thought the kid deserved a chance to try out with the more established Lincolns. Or, more emphatically, that The Lincolns needed him.

"So, what do you think? You wanna take a shot?" Brian asked Frank in the school corridor, as though it was no big deal. Devil-may-care was the absolute essence of Chisholm.

"Sure," answered a startled Frank, feeling his breath disappear and his knees wobble. After all, The Lincolns were the top band in town. "Yes, I mean. Should I—should we—we should rehearse, shouldn't we?"

Brian looked at Frank with amusement. "Nah! Just show up two nights from now in the cellar of the IGA store at the corner of Prince and Pleasant Streets. If it works, it works. If it doesn't, it doesn't. All right?"

"All right," agreed Frank, shaking his head. He liked singing with The Corvettes, but to sing with The Lincolns—well, that would be a whole different level.

As we have seen, Frank MacKay more than measured up. Without any rehearsal—in fact, without any idea which song or songs he would be asked to perform—Frank went up onstage at the Pleasant Street Hall and stood before the microphone. He had come with a list of the songs he knew and liked, but no one asked him for it. Instead, right away he heard drummer Rod Norrie begin the count for Little Richard's "Good Golly, Miss Molly."

In Frank's own words: "Figuring it was all-or-nothing time, I jumped in feet first. I screamed my way to the sax solo halfway through the tune. As Layne blasted his way through that mini twelve-bar break, I felt a rush like never before. I knew immediately that *together* we were tapping into something very special."

The Lincolns felt the same way about the kid in Grade 10. Frank MacKay stayed at the microphone the rest of the night, and at the end the crowd demanded two encores. Frank Mumford's recollection was that the younger Frank "sang a few Fats Domino tunes and blew us all away. We asked him to join our band." Nearly six decades later, in late 2018, Rod Norrie recalled: "We called Frank the next day and fired the a-holes who were giving us shit all the time. They really were assholes, lording it over us, making our lives miserable. Even the police were jubilant. They didn't like those guys at all. They wouldn't even let them in the Pleasant Street dance hall the next week because they'd heard we had a new singer. Frank MacKay played with us after that. He was such a great singer, he really was."

Layne Francis echoed Rod: "We were stunned by his amazing voice and talent. He freaked everyone out all those years ago, as he continued through the years. He was an amazing guy. I'm so proud to have played with him all the many years. Without Frank, it would have never happened." The *it* Layne was referring to was the renown and admirers The Lincolns would go on to earn over the decades that followed.

As soon became apparent, Frank MacKay brought a lot more into the band than simple raw talent. He developed into the consummate performer, always working on his singing and demanding the absolute best out of each of the other Lincolns—or any other group of musicians he ever played with. As Don Muir, fellow Lincoln and fellow Soma member, remarked at the May 2019 celebration of MacKay's life, "Frank worked harder than anyone at honing his craft."

Until age eleven, when he moved to Truro, Frank MacKay (born in 1944) grew up in a mining family in Stellarton. A family of eight, the MacKays lived in the Red Row neighbourhood, so-called because the coal company had painted the entire line of former company houses that colour. The boy's childhood was far from idyllic: money was tight, and his father, John James MacKay, had problems with gambling. And then his father lost an arm

Thirteen-year-old Frank MacKay (right, in white sports coat) and his brother Alan at the wedding of older brother John; it was around this time that Frank wrote "She is True," later a Lincolns staple.
(COURTESY OF FRANK MACKAY)

in an accident, after which there was more domestic strife and sometimes physical abuse. Understandably troubled, young Frank sought escape and comfort in music. He played a little piano and sometimes sang, but he was so shy that he would sing only when he was out of sight, hiding behind the piano. His younger sister, Rosaria, recalled in 2019 that at that young age Frank especially liked to sing the children's classic song "The Cat Came Back."

When Frank's father died in 1957, his mother, Florence, moved him and Rosaria to Truro. The two children went to St. Mary's, a Roman Catholic school that went up to Grade 9. Frank's attraction to music deepened the older he got and the more he listened to the radio and the 45s he occasionally bought. At age thirteen, Frank penned his first song, "She is True," which he later would sing from time to time with The Lincolns.

The performer Frank most admired during his early teens was Fats Domino, but he could also sing like Little Richard and other artists. His powerful and distinctive voice did not go unnoticed in a small town like Truro. Frank participated in a few singing events at St. Mary's, and his talent eventually caught the ears of the guys in The Corvettes. No longer as shy as he had once been—or at least now able to stand up onstage and perform before an audience—Frank agreed to sing with them. In late 2018 Frank recalled the very first gig he did with that initial band. "It was at a junior high in Bible Hill, and my take-home pay was eight quarters.... That was a large amount in those days," he said with a laugh.

Frank MacKay was not long with The Corvettes before joining The Lincolns in the fall of 1961. And since there were now two Franks in the group, each began to be identified within the band by their last name only, either Mumford or MacKay. And now, with a bona fide singer finally part of the band, the group felt it was time for a photo shoot. Their choice for an outfit in 1961 was casual, compared with the full suits and ties most of the bands on TV were dressing in. The Lincolns's look at the time was dark trousers, white shirts, and dark vests, without any sports jackets or ties. Wherever they performed that year, that was how The Lincolns presented themselves.

It was not long after Frank MacKay became a Lincoln that the other guys in the band decided their new singer needed an orientation of a different kind. That adventure began one evening as the band's new singer was coming out of George's restaurant. A blare from Layne Francis's car horn caught his attention. The 1959 blue Plymouth Fury was parked beside the Pleasant Street Hall. Frank quickly crossed Prince Street to see what was up. Into Layne's car he climbed.

"Ever been down to Murray Dorrington's?" Layne asked.

Frank shook his head.

The Lincolns's first look, in the Pleasant Street Hall circa 1961, shortly after Frank MacKay joined the band. Left to right: Brian Chisholm, Frank Mumford, Frank MacKay, Rod Norrie, and Layne Francis.
(PRIDHAM'S STUDIO)

"Hold onto your seat!"

Five minutes later Frank was in a part of Truro he had never seen: the westernmost portion of Prince Street, where it dead-ended alongside a portion of the Truro golf course. Officially, it was West Prince Street; unofficially, it was "the Island," one of three areas where people of African descent lived at the time.

Layne parked the car and led his younger fellow Lincoln to the door of a small bungalow. The sax player knocked. To Frank's great surprise, the door was opened by Lincoln drummer Rod Norrie. Next he saw Frank Mumford and Brian Chisholm further inside the house. The whole band was there! Frank started to speak, but Brian shushed him and pointed to the far side of the room. Frank looked across the crowded parlour and felt

The Murray Dorrington Trio: Wilfrid Connors on drums, Goby Chase on guitar, and Murray Dorrington at the piano.
(COURTESY OF HELEN DORRINGTON-PRICE)

his jaw drop. There was a jam session underway, and all four musicians were Black. Frank felt like he had entered a secret nightclub, a room filled with joyful sounds such as he imagined he would hear in New Orleans.

Frank, recall, was just seventeen, and his fellow Lincolns ranged in age from eighteen to twenty-one. Truro, moreover, was a "dry" town then: no bars within town limits and no restaurants licensed to sell alcohol. Anyone twenty-one or older who wished to buy beer or spirits had to go to a Nova Scotia Liquor Commission outlet during business hours—or to a bootlegger. Not surprisingly, a number of individuals were practising the latter trade, including Murray Dorrington, into whose house Layne Francis had just brought Frank MacKay.

Frank would soon learn the names of the musicians before him: Wilfred Connors on drums, Clint Halfkenny on guitar, Murray Dorrington on lead vocals, and second singer Max

Halfkenny, Clint's brother. All four were mature men, more than three times the ages of The Lincolns. Max's voice was the deepest bass Frank had ever heard. He thought the pictures on the wall surely rattled every time Max Halfkenny went deep. It was as if he were a human bass. To which point, with a laugh, Brian Chisholm said: "That guy imitates a bass guitar better than I play one."

The first impression seared into Frank MacKay's memory was the showmanship of drummer Wilfred Connors. All he had was a snare, hi-hat, and cymbal, but he put on a riveting show as he "worked it" with brushes instead of sticks. At one point, he left his seat and spent a feverish five minutes circling the cymbal with his brushes, over and over again. Frank couldn't believe what he was seeing.

Next, it was guitarist Clint Halfkenny's turn to blow Frank's mind. Clint moved seamlessly through a medley of songs from the late 1940s and early 1950s, taking the drummer with him through all the changes. "He was also all over the neck of the guitar with left-hand finger placements that had me completely mesmerized. I whispered to Frank Mumford, 'What's he doing?' Frank replied: 'The man grew up listening to jazz. Those are *passing chords* he's using.'"

The final member of the quartet was Murray Dorrington. Young Frank MacKay was awestruck by Murray's velvet voice and his ability to maintain pitch as each new song transitioned into its own key. Frank recalls: "Murray closed the medley with a rousing version of 'When the Saints Go Marching In.' It made us all feel like we were in the middle of Bourbon Street during Mardi Gras."

The quartet played for about an hour, then took a break. That was when Murray Dorrington came up to say hello to Layne and the other Lincolns.

Murray: "Hey Layne, where you been hiding? Ain't seen you in a while."

MURRAY DORRINGTON (1916-76)

The world is filled with people who make important contributions without receiving the publicity they deserve. In the Nova Scotia music world from the late 1940s to the 1960s, Murray Dorrington was such a person. He was born and raised in Truro, third oldest of eight children, and he grew up loving music. While in school, he entered the Truro Music Festival each year and usually came home with a trophy. As an adult, he sang as well as played piano, organ, bass, and drums. Yet because he was Black in an era with a racial divide, his name was little known beyond the Black community. Nonetheless, he and his fellow musicians were a major influence on The Lincolns.

Murray Dorrington also served his country, as a sergeant in the Canadian Army during the Second World War. Back home in Canada after the war, he married Alice Jean Williams in 1948. They adopted six-month-old Helen in 1953. One of Murray's proudest musical accomplishments was as a member of the Zion United Baptist Church Quartet (composed of Murray Dorrington, Harold Dorrington, Claude Jordan, and Walter Tynes). In 1965, the quartet represented Nova Scotia at the Dominion Day celebrations in Ottawa.

Layne: "Murray, I want you to meet Frank. He's the new singer with The Lincolns."

Murray: "Hey Frank, how ya doin'? You boys want a beer?"

Layne: "You bet. Frank?"

Frank: "Uh, okay...."

Murray: "I'll be right back."

Layne: "This is one of my favourite places to come. Always great musicians hangin' out here."

Murray: "Here you go, boys," handing over a few beers.

Layne: "Mur, you sing 'My Buddy' yet?"

Murray: "'My Buddy'? You like that old chestnut, don't ya? You ask for it every time you're here. You bring your horn? You wanna play?"

Layne: "No, but I really would like Frank to hear you sing that song."

Murray: "Well, hey, why not? Clint—gimme the key for 'My Buddy,' will you?"

Clint Halfkenny did as he was requested, then wrapped his arms around his guitar and brought the instrument to his chest. Then he, Max, and Wilfred fell silent, as did the entire house. The buzz of laughter and conversations just stopped. Frank was sure you could hear a pin drop. Sitting on the arm of a sofa, eyes closed, Murray Dorrington sang a cappella the song that Layne had requested.

"My Buddy" is a song of loss, written by Walter Donaldson and Gus Kahn in 1922 and sung since then by many dozens of artists. Its melancholy melody and lyrics touch listeners, without revealing specifically who the missed person is. Frank MacKay had never heard the song. As he listened to Murray Dorrington interpret it, he pictured who that lost buddy was for him. Then it came to him: it was someone different for every person in the room. Frank understood there was a lesson in that. "A great song, interpreted by a great singer, is never limited in its reach and meaning." The singer's job is not to stand up there and scream it out, but to sing the words like he's reliving an experience.

Visits to that West Prince Street address—to drink up both the atmosphere and the talents of Murray Dorrington and his musician friends, as well as a few seventy-five-cent beers—would be a regular part of The Lincolns's experience for many more years. The beer, by the way, then came mostly in quarts (nearly three times as much liquid as today's beer bottles). That the music played there was not rock 'n' roll, and that the musicians were much older than the guys in the band, did not deter the attraction at all. It was great music played by singers and players who inspired by their example.

Layne Francis recalled in 2018 that he and the other Lincolns "did a lot of jamming at Murray Dorrington's. It really helped define the band. Their playing and especially their singing was truly unreal. You had to hear it. It was so incredible."

Typically, The Lincolns went to Murray's late on Friday nights, after the dance at the Legion ended. But they also sometimes went for a visit and a quick beer during intermission, then headed back to the Legion for the second half of their performance. Their fifteen-minute intermissions were rarely that—they were closer to half an hour. One night, Danny Joseph and his buddies followed the band as they headed off at intermission. The would-be spies picked up a bottle of cheap wine for themselves from another bootlegger in "the Island," then walked on to Murray Dorrington's, where they'd seen The Lincolns enter. Inside Murray's place was a show Danny and his friends would never forget. Murray Dorrington was at the piano, with Wilfred Connors on drums, Frank MacKay singing, and everyone in the packed house was grooving along to what Danny figured was "Southern Gospel R & B."

Frank MacKay, Layne Francis, Murray Dorrington, and Don Muir at the Truro Golf Club, circa 1966.

From the vantage point of 2018, Frank MacKay described Murray Dorrington as his mentor, and thanked him for the "vocal master classes at UMD, the University of Murray Dorrington." The affection was mutual. Lukey Maxwell, who grew up in "the Island" close to Murray Dorrington, recalled in 2019 that, when it came to The Lincolns, "Mur just loved them guys. He loved The Lincolns."

Frank MacKay and Layne Francis were not the only ones in the band to find inspiration and useful practical tips at Murray Dorrington's. Rod Norrie grew as a drummer watching Wilfred Connors do his thing, and Brian Chisholm and Frank Mumford learned more than a few tricks from Clint Halfkenny. Occasionally, Black musicians from the USA stopped in to Murray's place for a few beers and to jam. Sometimes The Lincolns chanced to be there to further expand their musical education. On one occasion, a visiting American guitarist showed Frank Mumford ways to play their common instrument. The younger guitarist immediately incorporated the new techniques into how he played.

Visits by The Lincolns to Murray Dorrington's continued throughout the lifespan of the band, as testified to by Jack Lilly, who did not join the group until 1968.

The police never raided the place for illegal alcohol sales when The Lincolns were there, but such raids occurred from time to time. Anne Murray recalled hearing about "after-hours" incidents at Murray's place from Davey Wells, who sang with her on various CBC TV music shows. "Davey was a great storyteller and a very funny guy. He regaled us with stories about his time spent at Murray's. I remember one about the police showing up and the running around that ensued. The Murray quote that I heard most often was, 'You don't got to go home but you got to get outta here!'"

One evening, two of The Lincolns and a friend decided to prank Mur by pretending to be police making a raid. It happened like this, as retold by Don Muir. He, Frank MacKay, and Norm MacKenzie arrived at Murray Dorrington's place in Norm's car, which "had a speaker with a kind of old cop radio mic hooked up to it—the kind with the button on the side. There was quite a crowd at Mur's that night, when we pulled into the yard with the speaker blaring, 'Come out with your hands up, Dorrington—we know you're in there!' Mur stuck his head out the door and raised his hands and we started laughing. As did the people inside when they realized what had happened. Needless to say, Mur was quite pissed off at us but only for a few minutes, as we went in and joined the party."

The songs they played at dances bore no relation to the music The Lincolns enjoyed at Murray Dorrington's. At that West Prince Street address, the material tended to be easy listening

The Lincolns performing before a large crowd inside the Industrial Building at the Nova Scotia Provincial Exhibition, Bible Hill. Left to right: Brian Chisholm (seen from behind), Frank MacKay (at the mic), Layne Francis (holding his sax), Frank Mumford (playing guitar), and Rod Norrie (at the drums).

jazz tunes made popular by Nat King Cole, Louis Armstrong, and Frank Sinatra. At the dances, the band was all rock 'n' roll, featuring the contemporary hits and the classics from the fifties. Increasingly, it was singer Frank MacKay who picked the band's songlist. Some material suited his taste and vocal range better than others. Ray Charles soon became a favourite of his, after he began listening to Frank Mumford's collection of albums. The Lincolns started performing several of Charles's songs, including his 1961 hit "Unchain My Heart."

The teenagers dancing in front of The Lincolns in the early 1960s—think of boys with crewcuts and girls with billowing skirts thanks to puffy crinolines—were eager to try out the latest dance crazes from the United States. More often than not, those dances had been popularized by the TV show *American Bandstand*, which began as a local show out of Philadelphia in 1950, then went nationwide in 1957. In 1964, the program relocated to Los Angeles, where it remained for decades. Whether or not Truro teenagers could watch *American Bandstand* on their family living room TV sets in the early 1960s, they still heard about the latest dance craze and soon learned the steps.

Three dances in particular dominated the early 1960s: the Twist, the Mashed Potato, and the Monkey. All came out of African American origins, based on songs by Black recording artists. Those artists appeared on *American Bandstand*, yet the show's policy until 1964 was *not* to allow any Black teens to dance in the foreground. The producers worried that such a scene would be provocative at a time when segregation still existed in much of the United States, and feared they might lose sponsors. Only after the show moved to Los Angeles in February 1964 were Black dancers allowed front and centre on *American Bandstand*'s broadcast.

Obviously, in the Truro dance halls where The Lincolns were playing there were no TV cameras nor any sponsors worrying about who was dancing where or with whom. Young people, regardless of their background, could stand or dance wherever they felt most comfortable. Ideally, that was with others they knew, but on a crowded floor you had to take what limited space you could get. Based on surviving photos and people's recollections, it seems that most of the Black kids gravitated close to the stage wherever the band was playing.

Well, you might be wondering, if there wasn't any kind of official segregation at Lincolns dances, why bring up the topic of race at all? It's to remind us that, in 1960s Truro, as elsewhere in Nova Scotia, racial prejudice still limited where people of colour could go, live, and work. Dances were among the few activities—and public spaces—where everyone could attend and mingle, regardless of their skin colour. Nonetheless, sometimes

DANCE CRAZES OF THE EARLY SIXTIES

Hank Ballard wrote and recorded the original version of "The Twist" in 1959, but it was not until Chubby Checker released the same song in 1960 that it became a craze. Its spread was much enhanced when Checker performed it on *American Bandstand*. Next up was "The Mashed Potato." Its name and its moves were created by the great R & B recording artist James Brown in 1959, but it did not become a continent-wide craze until 1962, when The Contours had a massive hit for Motown Records entitled "Do You Love Me?" "The Mashed Potato" was mentioned in the lyrics. The following year, 1963, a new dance called "The Monkey" was the next big thing. Once again, its origins were in rhythm and blues, in songs by Major Lance as well as by The Miracles. Other dance crazes included "The Fly," "The Pony," The Swim," and "The Watusi."

the racial tensions that existed in the world beyond the dance hall doors did come to the surface.

According to those who attended dances at the Truro Legion in the late 1960s, some of the scuffles and fights that occurred there were between combatants whose different-coloured skin was reason enough to come to blows. The fights, of course, had nothing to do with the musicians onstage, who were joyfully playing music made by people from every background. On one occasion in the early 1960s, when The Lincolns were playing at the Provincial Exhibition in Bible Hill, an instance of interracial dating led to the stabbing in the abdomen of a young Black man out on the dance floor. The victim fell to the floor with a bluish circle of blood showing on his shirt. "She stabbed him, she stabbed him!" bass player Brian Chisholm shouted in panic and shock.

Truth be told, the story behind the incident is much more complicated than it first appears. The victim, who survived, was a Truro boxer married to a woman from the same Black community in which he lived. But it was no secret that he was also dating a white woman. Recalls Rod Norrie: "His wife was mad as hell. Talk was all over town and everybody was wondering what was going to happen if he came to the dance and danced with his white girlfriend." Well, they soon found out.

The hall was electric in anticipation. Sure enough, as feared, the boxer danced with his white girlfriend to the sound of The Lincolns. Out of a group of Black women at the back of the hall came the offended wife, who took a swing at her cheating husband. The boxer stopped dancing and defended himself while he protected his girlfriend. Then came his wife's sister, who swung her purse at him with one hand and, flashing a knife in the other, struck him in the abdomen.

The hall was in pandemonium: the band stopped playing, and the police arrived and tried to restore order. But for Rod Norrie, it was time to pee. The band was known to enjoy a few beers while playing, and he simply had to get to the washroom. The police, however, were refusing to let anyone out, and Rod couldn't wait. It was a tight fit—one he couldn't do today—but he squeezed his then slender frame through the small admission window at the entrance and made his call of nature.

The stabbing was the talk of the town for some time, reducing the numbers attending Lincolns dances for a while.

On one of the band's many road trips away from Truro, The Lincolns were confronted by an example of undeniable racism, which they dealt with straight on. Arriving in the Nova Scotia town in question in the early evening, they proceeded to the hall where they were to play. The owner of the venue took one look at some Black kids milling around outside the hall in anticipation of the dance and announced to the band that "*They* are not allowed in here."

The Lincolns looked at each other with startled faces, then took a breath. This guy was obviously a throwback to a racist era that was finally beginning to be thrust aside. More than that, some of the kids the fellow was referring to were friends of guys in the band. As Rod Norrie observed in 2018 about this incident: "Friends don't turn their back on friends." The band replied at once with a single voice: "If they don't get in, we don't play." The owner didn't like it, but all he could do was shake his head. He had no choice but to back down. The Lincolns played that night, and everyone who wanted to come into the hall did so, with no exceptions. In such simple ways, however slowly, Nova Scotia advanced toward a more open and inclusive society.

The colour-blind example set by The Lincolns was rooted in the band's taste in music. They loved artists who could play at a high level, especially those who did so with a lot of feeling. Frank MacKay recalled that when The Lincolns played in the Halifax area, they sometimes went to the Arrows Club in the city's North End for a late-night visit. Black R & B musicians from elsewhere in Canada and from the USA played there regularly, and Frank said "some were incredible singers and musicians." The guys would talk to those players after their sets and invite them to come to Truro the next day. Some did, and spent a good portion of a Sunday afternoon jamming at the Legion with The Lincolns. One visiting musician whom Frank described as "astonishing" and "amazing" was William "Smitty" Smith, who played with Eric Mercury's band.

Looking back from the perspective of 2018, Helen Dorrington-Price, daughter of Murray Dorrington, feels strongly that, during The Lincolns's 1961–69 period, the group played an important role in scattering the old prejudices of mistrust, fear, and hate. Whether it was on purpose or by accident, "the band was a great influence in changing people's attitudes. The music they played—soul music—broke down barriers. They respected the Black musicians." Close friend Sherry O'Brien agrees: "The Lincolns brought the two cultures together."

The Lincolns were popular in the Truro area right from their start in 1961, but in 1962 the five-man band decided they needed a bigger and better sound. They wanted a sixth member. Of course, any additional person would reduce each individual's share of the money coming in from appearances, but that was not thought the least bit important. The most important goal for the band was to have the best possible sound. It's why they bought the best Fender amplifiers and why they chose to add another horn, a second saxophone. The choice of who that player should be naturally fell to Layne Francis.

Layne's selection was Lee Taylor, whose name we encountered earlier as lead guitarist with The Corvettes. Taylor could also play the sax and owned a tenor model. As Layne Francis tells the story, he never considered anyone other than Lee. "He was always hanging around the band, and he could play."

Lee Taylor (1945–68) grew up just outside Truro on Harmony Road and was still living with his parents and going to Central Colchester High School when he began playing with the band. As is apparent in every photo of the band taken at that time, Lee was short and slight. After he shifted from tenor to baritone sax, his instrument was almost as tall as he was. Lee had to sit

Dancers up close to the stage at the Pleasant Street Hall, 1966; all six Lincolns at that time are visible: (left to right) Lee Taylor, Layne Francis, Don Muir, Frank MacKay, Frank Mumford, and Rod Norrie, as well as dancers (left to right) Linda Jackson, Lane Clyke, Gayle Paris, Ethel "Tinkle" MacDonald, Glenda Talbot, and Joanne Tynes. (PRIDHAM'S STUDIO)

on a pillow to see out the windshield of every car he drove. Band members estimated he weighed somewhere between ninety and a hundred pounds, but Don Muir maintained that, on his scale, Lee measured only eighty-five. Not that his height and weight mattered. What counted was that when his sax was added to Layne's, it gave The Lincolns a powerhouse sound, distinct from every other band in the Maritimes in the 1960s. No other Nova Scotia band at the time even thought of having a baritone sax in the mix.

Fine sax player though Lee Taylor was, Rod Norrie recalls that he was shy about being in the limelight alongside the older and more renowned Layne Francis. Rod remembers how Layne frequently used to nudge Lee closer to the microphone so that

Lee Taylor soloing on sax at the Truro Legion, 1966; Frank MacKay is playing the Farfisa organ. (**PRIDHAM'S STUDIO**)

the glory sound of their two saxes would be at its maximum. Eventually, the band bought another mic, one for each horn.

There are two other details about Lee Taylor to mention here. The first is that he liked speed—in the form of motorbikes and fast cars. One of his friends, Colin Topshee, recalled that Lee absolutely loved his BSA and Triumph bikes, and later, "his bright yellow, brand new 396 Chevelle." Seeing tiny Lee Taylor on a big bike was quite a sight. He used to offer to take Rod Norrie for a ride on his BSA, but the Lincolns's drummer always declined. Except once, when he got on the bike in front of the Legion, and Lee proceeded to do a wheelie all the way up Exhibition Street. Rod hung on for dear life, and when it was over, vowed never to ride with Lee again. Don Muir, on the other hand, often used to get on the back of Lee's BSA. Since Lee was so slight, Don recalled in 2019, "he wasn't heavy enough to start his bike. I used to have to kick-start it for him."

The second detail to know about Lee Taylor is that he had suffered from diabetes since he was a small child. Back then, diabetes was an extremely serious condition that required insulin injections. Lee's condition would claim his life far too soon, but for the moment, let's concentrate on life being lived to its fullest, which was Lee Taylor's philosophy as well as the essence of going to an early 1960s Lincolns dance.

Whether you caught them at a high school or on a university campus, or in Truro at the underground Pleasant Street Hall, The Lincolns's brand of music up to 1964 was pretty much guaranteed to get you involved. In the opinion of Layne Francis, someone who by 2018 had been playing music professionally for more than sixty years, The Lincolns had something special right from the start. "The great thing about the band was the great *feel* we had—and always had."

One venue the band played a few times was in Bible Hill, at the Nova Scotia Agricultural College (NSAC, now the Agricultural Campus of Dalhousie University). Bob Grant was a student at the NSAC from the fall of 1962 until the spring of 1964. What stands out in his memory of the Lincolns dances he attended are three details. First, "their music was terrific." Second, "we used to marvel at the rum bottles that were left after the shows." And third, "Roddie Norrie was a bit of a celebrity as the drummer and a member of a noteworthy Liberal family."

Let's leave aside the rum bottles and Rod's family's politics, and focus instead on Bob Grant's comment that "their music was terrific." I view that as an assessment of two separate factors: the choice of songs the band presented and the professionalism (and entertainment value) of the playing. Even at this early date, The

Lincolns could engage a crowd and wow them with their presentation of music made for dancing.

In 1963, the group learned of the passing of Peter Harris, in whose basement the original nucleus of the band had begun back in 1959. Peter was an original Lincoln, and his death hit the group hard. He was not only their age, he was also someone who shared their musical aspirations and dreams. He was like a brother to Rod Norrie, Frank Mumford, and Brian Chisholm. In late 2018, fifty-five years after the fact, Rod Norrie recalls getting the phone call from Frank Mumford telling him that Peter had died in a car crash in Maine. Rod was stunned, recalling his own accident in Maine, when he broke his leg. Peter had not been at the wheel but a passenger—asleep in the back seat. "How hard it hit us," said Rod, who compared hearing the news about Peter to that year's assassination of John F. Kennedy for the impact it had on him. "I still think about Peter many times, especially at the reunions."

There would be more sad times ahead for the band, but this is not yet the place to speak of them. Instead, let's say something about the life each Lincoln led apart from the band.

Once they left high school, all members either found jobs or went off to university before moving into the workforce. Although The Lincolns were steadily earning renown, the money coming in was never enough to make anybody rich. The guys had to have Monday-to-Friday jobs as well—jobs that allowed them to play Friday and Saturday nights and practice new songs on Sunday afternoons.

Drummer Rod Norrie was the first in the band to pursue higher education. In the fall of 1960, he enrolled in business classes at Mount Allison University in Sackville, New Brunswick. That was where his mother had been a professor and where she would later serve on the board of governors. (His older sister

Margaret, when known as Margaret McCain, would go on to become chancellor of the university.)

Rod is the first to admit that he did not take his courses as seriously as he should have. One distraction was sports. Because of that interest, and the fact that he was one of the few students on campus with a car—a brown '59 Chevy he describes as "the ugliest car in the world"—Rod was asked to be the manager of the Mount A basketball team. He and the coach transported the team to off-campus games. Rod's primary focus, however, was on getting home every weekend to play with The Lincolns. Those many treks made him familiar with every turn and straight stretch on the early 1960s highway between Sackville and Truro, long before there were any four-lane, twinned highways. One thing and one thing only, impassable driving conditions on the Tantramar Marsh because of a snowstorm, kept Rod away from playing with The Lincolns. When that happened, the band had to find a substitute drummer for the night.

Dave Gass, of the short-lived Corvettes, remembers getting the occasional call to sit in with The Lincolns in early 1963. Gass didn't have a drum set of his own but was allowed to use Rod's kit. Thinking back on those evenings, he said: "I was more than happy to be the fill-in for Roddie. I don't recall that we did much practising aside from running through some songs prior to playing. It was learn as you go.... Playing at Hopgoods was quite an experience. Frank was a showman, and he and Layne would go into the crowd with Layne on Frank's shoulders."

Dave doesn't mention it, but I should add that Layne was playing his sax while on Frank's shoulders. At other times, Frank would put the much smaller and lighter Lee Taylor on his shoulders, with Lee playing his huge baritone horn. Such excursions down off the stage and weaving in and around the dancers were always crowd favourites.

Another part of Dave Gass's experience as a substitute drummer with The Lincolns related to the drinking. In Gass's words: "The occasional quart or two of warm Schooner was consumed prior to some performances, and on one occasion I overdid it playing at a house party. My parents were not impressed. My dad was a United Church minister in Bible Hill. I don't think he forbade me from further performing, but I don't recall many sessions with The Lincolns after that. Roddie was back from Mount A shortly after for the summer and I was off to Mount A in the fall of 1963."

Sometime later, Dave Gass was down in the audience as The Lincolns, with Rod Norrie back in his customary seat, performed on campus at Mount A. "It was quite a show," said Dave wistfully.

What had brought the band to play at Mount Allison in the first place, a few years earlier, was a request from Rod Norrie's fellow students in his residence. They wondered if he could get his Truro band to play for a fundraiser during the 1963 winter carnival. The Lincolns said yes and proceeded to delight the students with their trademark intensity. The college kids packed the old gym where the band played, some students literally sitting up in and hanging on to the rafters. One of those in the crowd was Lynn MacMurtery Schnare, from Truro. Nearly six decades after those performances, she recalled: "I remember this *so* well. All of us from Truro were so excited to have our hometown band come play for us. Truro was proud of them, and Mount A was about to find out why. Upon seeing Frank MacKay, I literally jumped into his arms. He swung me around and we laughed and laughed. Their music made everyone get up and dance. Yay for rock 'n' roll! The Lincolns were the absolute best!"

In the years to come, the band would play at Mount A many more times, and the band always loved it. The students were so responsive.

The contract for The Lincolns to perform at Mount Allison in February 1963 still exists. It specifies that the band was to be paid $300 for three separate shows over three days totalling six and a quarter hours. That's the equivalent of $2,400 today, or $400 each. It seemed like fair pay at the time, but it was nowhere near enough for anyone to live on. It supplemented the income the guys were making in their day jobs, that's all. Later appearances by the band at Mount A did not generate contracts; the students knew that once the band had given its word to appear they would be there, no matter how challenging the winter driving conditions.

Like Rod Norrie, Brian Chisholm eventually also went off to university. In his case, it was Saint Mary's University in Halifax to obtain a degree in education. Before that, he worked wherever he could to make enough money to get by. Meanwhile, Frank Mumford got a job in the insurance industry, eventually moving into a very senior position in Halifax. Layne Francis worked at a Nova Scotia Liquor Commission outlet in Truro, while Frank MacKay helped out at the Hatfield's corner store his sister owned. Lee Taylor, after leaving high school, worked as the timekeeper (looking after the payroll) for Tidewater Construction in the Windsor area. Clearly, the guys in The Lincolns had their feet firmly planted on the ground, except on the weekends, when they soared as musicians before admiring crowds. They had come a long way in the half-dozen years since they got their first drums, guitars, and horns.

Of all The Lincolns during the early 1960s, Brian Chisholm turns up in more tales than anyone else. More often than not it is his devil-may-care attitude and sense of humour that are highlighted. Those two qualities sometimes got him into trouble.

Everyone agrees that Chisholm was a great showman on a stage, but every so often he would do something that left the other guys in the band shaking their heads. Like standing on top of an amp to attract a crowd of girls during a show at Mount A. Or putting down his guitar and abruptly leaving the stage in the middle of a song. Or, one night, insisting that the entire band wear Hawaiian shirts, and then later seen outside bare-chested, jumping up and down on his Hawaiian shirt in a mud puddle, angry about something. Then there was the early morning hour at Rod Norrie's place when Brian woke up everyone in the house by turning up the volume on the stereo as high as it would go and playing, over and over, by lifting the needle back to the beginning, the "1, 2, 3, 4" start of The Beatles's "I Saw Her Standing There." Brian thought it was hilarious. Everyone else, not so much.

One day, Rod Norrie recalled, Chisholm was in the back seat of Rod's car, which was parked in front of George's restaurant in Truro, when Brian made a mocking remark to a well-known tough guy and ex-con (and sometime musician) who was walking past. What Brian intended as a joke was taken as an insult. The ex-con demanded Brian get out of the car, which Brian immediately did, utterly unafraid. An instant later, Chisholm was on his back. With his fist drawn back ready to pound Brian, the tough guy looked up to see Rod and Frank Mumford outside the car with their arms crossed, shaking their heads. It was warning enough. The fellow let Chisholm go. The incident, however, had no effect on Brian. He continued to say whatever, whenever, to whomever, regardless of the consequences. It was a quality his fellow Lincolns both worried about and loved about him.

Another story involves the first car Brian bought. The band's gigs were putting spending money in all their pockets, and Chisholm used some of his to pick up a four-door Dodge DeSoto for fifty dollars. Before then, the other band members had had to drive Brian everywhere. So, when he showed up at rehearsal one day and announced, "I bought a car," everyone laughed. But it was true. Rod Norrie described Chisholm's DeSoto as "plush as a boat on wheels. And old. It was obviously on its last legs." Nonetheless, Brian loved having a car of his own. He gave rides to anybody who would get in, though not many dared. Brian didn't have a licence or insurance and had never driven anything before. Plus, his focus was not always on the road. But to those who did climb in, driving with Brian Chisholm was an adventure.

The DeSoto delighted Brian until one day it died. When that happened, Brian, lacking the money to fix it, did something few would consider: he pulled a rifle out of the trunk and shot the car. Later, he told the other Lincolns what he had done. "'I put it out of its misery,'" Rod Norrie recalled Brian's saying. "'I shot it and it made a long ooh. Ooh!' And then he laughed like hell." The *ooh* sound Brian imitated was the air coming out of the bullet-ridden tires. "Only Brian," said Rod, shaking his head.

By 1964, The Lincolns had many fans, and not just in Truro. Across the province, at high school dances and on college campuses, fans could not wait for them to put on a show. In part, the appeal was the particular songs The Lincolns played. They were tunes with a strong beat and captivating rhythm that made people want to dance. But it wasn't just that. It was also how the band *performed* those songs, in its own distinctive way. The Lincolns brought familiar songs to life and turned them into the best versions the crowd had ever heard. A Lincolns version was not always two or three minutes long like the radio single—it could be double or triple that length to keep the dancing going.

The Lincolns's appeal was equally the energy that everyone onstage put into their playing. The band simply loved performing before dancing crowds. There was reciprocity: the band put everything into each song, the energy went out to the dancers, and the dancers sent it back up to the musicians onstage. It made for a bond between performers and audience. Or an equation, if you like, that looked like this: We are theirs = They are ours.

Rod Norrie expressed it a little differently: "Everyone was having fun. That was what made The Lincolns."

In 2018, as I was starting to work on this book, several Lincolns told me essentially the same thing: "We were better collectively than the sum of our individual parts." Maybe so. Or maybe that pithy statement humbly underestimates the talents and musicianship of the guys up onstage. Besides, I have it on pretty good authority that it's the "sum of the parts" that matters most. In fact, it's all that counts. Here is what The Boss said during his 2018 *Springsteen on Broadway* Netflix performance: "Bands are all about what happens to musicians who go in search of lightning and thunder. They come together in a whole that is greater than the sum of their parts. They may not be the best players; that is not necessary. They need to be the right players, and when they play together there is a communion of souls. In a real band, principles of math get stood on their head, and one plus one equals three." That's as good a description of The Lincolns as I have ever heard. I'm pretty sure Bruce would have loved the Truro band.

I am also inclined to offer a comparison with two much better known bands, which came off poorly in comparison with The Lincolns. In the spring of 1968, Craig Stanfield and I caught a show in Fort Lauderdale, Florida, that featured The Beach Boys and Buffalo Springfield (with Neil Young and Stephen Stills). There before us—less than fifty feet away in a small venue—were bands with multiple hit records. Yet I barely recall the performances at all. No one onstage appeared to care about the audience at all; they were mailing in their songs from somewhere far away. It was nothing like a Lincolns dance, where there was

Turning Pink
and Shovelling Snow

One of the many jobs Brian Chisholm had was at Hub Beverages in Bible Hill, a business owned by his stepfather, Harold Bates. Hub produced soft drinks in a wide range of colours and sweet tastes: orange, root beer, lime, and cherry, to name the most popular. The large vats where all the ingredients were mixed and stirred were located in the basement. As always, Brian said what came to him the moment it popped into his head. One day, something he said was the last straw for his co-workers at Hub Beverages. They picked him up and tossed him into one of the vats: clothes, boots, gloves, and all. It turned out to be the vat filled with cherry pop. "He was pink for a week," Rod Norrie related. "He wasn't in long, but it all soaked into his skin. And, of course, he had to tell everyone what had happened—his latest escapade."

Another time, the band was in Stewiacke, Nova Scotia, when their car became stuck in a snowdrift. They all got out to see what they could do, including Chisholm, who exited with an old guitar he hated because it wouldn't stay tuned. He tried to use the guitar as a shovel on the drift, but it was next to impossible. So Brian stood straight up and threw the instrument as far as he could off into the night. "He was fun to have around," said Rod Norrie in 2018. "Always entertaining. You never knew what to expect."

always electricity in the air. Collectively and individually, the band exuded charisma. They loved what they were doing and invited the audience to join in the fun.

Drummer Rod Norrie stated that the band really liked performing at familiar venues, but there was another dynamic when they went somewhere for the first time. "It was great. We'd have new people to entertain, new people to make dance. We'd do our best to make them want to have us back again."

By January 1964, The Lincolns had established a tight band with a trademark sound and a growing audience. Who knew what lay ahead? How far they could go...if in fact they wanted to go anywhere other than exactly where they were, which was playing around Nova Scotia and New Brunswick with Truro as their home base.

Well, no one ever really knows what's in the tea leaves or crystal ball. But for The Lincolns, as January 1964 came to a close, the future seemed luminously bright. The six guys in the band were still only in their late teens and early twenties. Bigger audiences had to be around the corner, along with bigger paydays. Isn't that how it worked? And when those bigger days arrived, maybe the band would write some of their own songs? Get a manager, someone who would help steer the course ahead? Maybe roadies to help with the gear? Why, maybe they would even....

Whatever that next thought was, we can leave it incomplete. That's because after January 1964 came February, and unlike other Februarys, the one that year reconfigured the musical world in a single night. That was the Sunday evening, February 9, The Beatles performed live on TV across North America before an audience of seventy-three million. Among those watching the *Ed Sullivan Show* that night were The Lincolns. One of them, Doreen Woodworth recollected, was Frank Mumford, her boyfriend at the time. As a lark, Frank and his brother John wet and combed down their hair to watch the broadcast, their foreheads covered Beatles-style.

In the weeks that followed, the once-beckoning future of The Lincolns grew complicated, then dim. How quickly their lives had changed.

3
NOW
WHAT?
1964–65

U *nless you were alive at the time, it might be hard to believe just how* massive the impact of The Beatles was in 1964. Before their appearance on the *Ed Sullivan Show* on three successive Sunday evenings in February that year, some Beatles songs were already popular. After those appearances, with truly massive TV audiences, *popular* was not a sufficiently strong term. Hordes of screaming fans and an unprecedented domination of record sales had already led the British media to describe the phenomenon as "Beatlemania." A mania it truly was, with young people not just loving the music of the Fab Four—snapping up their 45s—but also purchasing magazines about them, Beatle wigs, lunch boxes bearing their images, and hundreds of other branded items.

For months, no one in the Western world could get enough of The Beatles. Newspapers and other media followed their every move, and their songs, and those of other "British Invasion" groups, took over the musical world. For live music bands such as The Lincolns, who played covers of what people wanted to hear, this rapid turn of events was a major challenge. For one thing, theirs was a band with two saxes, instruments The Beatles did not use. As Frank MacKay recalled, "we did our best to accommodate the craze" by performing several Beatles songs. In fact, The Lincolns had been performing a few Beatles songs before most people had even heard of the British group—songs that Frank MacKay had heard and liked. But after the appearance on the *Ed Sullivan Show*, people coming to the Pleasant Street Hall suddenly wanted "a dozen or more. It became obvious," Frank MacKay told me in late 2018, "that it wasn't going to work for us. My voice wasn't suited to the material, nor did we have the strong vocal harmonies the Liverpudlians had perfected." What The Lincolns offered versus what The Beatles sounded like were "two styles completely at odds."

For a few months, the Truro band did its best to play both the music they preferred and some of the new Beatles songs the crowd was demanding. The musicians practised the new material out at the Norrie family farm, and Rod felt that "we did a good job on them, we did." But people wanted more, and they wanted the sound to be like that on The Beatles's records.

By the time May rolled around, some of The Lincolns figured it was best to break up—Rod Norrie insists he was not of that opinion; he never wanted the group to split—or anyway take a pause. They had enjoyed three good years, but now, incredibly quickly, their kind of music was no longer what dancers were demanding. In Frank MacKay's words, "a decision was made to put the band on hold." Whether anyone seriously expected they would ever get back together again, I can't say—likely not. The lifespan of rock 'n' roll bands has always been notoriously short.

The Lincolns all went their separate ways. In singer Frank MacKay's case, "never having been out of Atlantic Canada before, the hiatus gave me a chance to visit my mother and sister who were living in Sarnia, Ontario, at the time." Ontario was also the eventual destination for bass player Brian Chisholm. First, he moved to Chicago, working with a Christmas tree company, then later relocated to St. Catharines, Ontario, with a handful of other guys from Truro. Along the way, Brian picked up the nickname "Chicago" to add to his already strong identity. Before he left Truro, Chisholm sold his 1961 Fender Precision bass and 1961 Fender Bassman amp to young fan Barry Ryan, who had begun playing with The Imperials.

Meanwhile, lead guitarist Frank Mumford settled in Halifax to further his day-job career in insurance, at which he was very good. That might seem to be the polar opposite from rock 'n' roll lead guitarist, but Frank Mumford made it work. With The Lincolns seeming to have come to an end, Mumford sold his 1961 Fender Jazzmaster guitar to the same Barry Ryan who had bought Chisholm's bass. (Barry no longer has either vintage instrument, as they were subsequently sold or traded away.)

For their part, saxophonist Layne Francis continued working at the Nova Scotia Liquor Commission in Truro and playing the odd gig, especially the jazz he loved, while younger sax player Lee Taylor kept working as the timekeeper for Tidewater Construction.

Drummer Rod Norrie returned to Truro from Mount Allison University in May 1964 to work in the family business, the Fundy Jersey Farm. He did occasionally play drums with local musicians such as piano player Ronnie Horne and Freddie Cormier, but he now had family responsibilities of his own. He had married Eleanor Tucker, mentioned earlier in this book, and their first child, Robin, was born in 1964. Two more children, Charlotte and Jacquelyn, were to come in the years that followed.

Each of the six *former* Lincolns retained a keen recollection of having been a member of that band. How could they not! They had enjoyed quite a run since 1961. But as the months after their break-up ticked by, and they all moved into 1965, that identity as a Lincoln was increasingly spoken of in the past tense: I *was* instead of I *am*.

Of the six Lincolns, the one whose 1964–65 story we know most about is that of Frank MacKay, who, you might recall, moved to Sarnia, Ontario, to visit his mother and sister. Sarnia, located on the easternmost shore of Lake Huron, right on the border with the United States, is about a two-hour drive from Detroit, home of Motown Records. In May 1964, when Frank arrived, Sarnia had a population of fifty thousand, or four times that of Truro. It was a city with a refinery, which put a definite petroleum tang into the air. "Despite the aroma," Frank recalled, "I took an instant liking to it."

Frank applied for various jobs and soon landed one in a grocery store called Walker Brothers (one of two Walker Brothers stores in the city). He had fibbed a little on his application, stating that he "had worked groceries in Nova Scotia. I didn't tell them that my experience consisted solely of holding the fort after school at my sister Marie's small neighbourhood convenience store." Frank worked hard at the grocery and fitted in "as a dependable employee who earned his paycheque." One benefit he particularly enjoyed was being in the stockroom at noon when the baked goods and sweets arrived. He would help the driver unload the trays and treat himself to a mint chocolate brownie or jumbo butter tart. Frank confesses: "I gained fifteen pounds my first month."

The summer of 1964 went by quickly as Frank settled into his new life in Sarnia. From time to time—well, almost daily—he wondered if his music career might be over, left behind in Truro. After all, at nineteen, he was getting old.

One Saturday in September, while Frank was having lunch at a café near the Walker Brothers store, he saw one of the younger employees come in. Frank recalled: "I signalled for him to join me." The kid was Brian Hill, seventeen-year-old nephew to the grocery store's manager. Brian told Frank he "was entering his second year of high school." More important, he "mentioned he played drums in a band. After that, no other topic arose, it was all about music. I told him I used to be a singer. (Oh, the drama! But when you're a teenager and haven't sung for four months, those months feel like years.)"

"You should drop by my house next week and check us out," said Brian Hill. "We rehearse every Wednesday night in my dad's rec room."

When Frank didn't respond right away, the seventeen-year-old laughed sarcastically. "Too good for us are ya, grandpa?"

Frank had to smile, recalling that he had been seventeen when he started with The Lincolns. That smile prompted Brian Hill to say: "So...my place next Wednesday at 7:30? As a matter of fact, I'll even come pick you up."

The following Wednesday evening, Frank was in Brian Hill's basement meeting the entire band, all his junior by a year or two: Tim Griffin (lead guitar), Gary Thompson (bass), and Ken Charrington (second guitar). No piano, no organ, and no horns— just the basic instruments used by The Beatles, The Rolling Stones, and all the other British groups.

To start things off, the group launched into The Ventures's classic, "Walk, Don't Run." The Lincolns had played the same tune a few hundred times, and to Frank's ears these kids' version "sounded pretty darn good. I applauded. Then it was time to find out if adding me to the mix was going to work or not." Frank suggested they try Ray Charles's "Unchain My Heart," a song he'd often sung with The Lincolns. Without any horns, Frank wondered how the song would sound in the hands of this Sarnia band. It turned out that lead guitarist Tim Griffin "made up for the lack of horns by adding some clever 'on the spot' background vocals, which the other players added to once they figured out what he was doing."

Frank's recollection is that "by the end of that first session, we had worked up seven or eight tunes, and as the weekly rehearsals continued, we soon had a set list of twenty-five or thirty songs." They called themselves The Strangers, and in January 1965 they had their first booking, at Tim Griffin's high school. It went well, "because the next thing you know we were playing schools all over town...and even did the Lambton County Saddle Club a time or two. Yee-haw! Good times, with good people."

Drummer Brian Hill recalled in 2019 just how good Frank was as a singer: "one of the very best I ever heard. Every band in Sarnia wanted him, once they heard him, but he chose to stay with The Strangers." Guitarist Tim Griffin, who would go on to have a long career as a professional musician, added that The Strangers won a Battle of the Bands contest over all the other bands "because we had Frank and they didn't." Much more important, Tim remembered that it was Frank who encouraged him to sing in front of a band. "He taught me the meaning of 'sing it like you mean it or give them their money back,' and 'play it like you mean it or give them their money back.' ...I've tried to play like that ever since that time. Thank you, Frank! His heart was as big and beautiful as his voice."

The months rolled by, the way they do when one is in a routine. In Frank MacKay's case, the routine was working at the grocery store during the day and practising or performing with his new band. It wasn't the same experience it had been with his old buddies in The Lincolns, but Frank was nonetheless pleased that he had shown he could adapt and was still singing.

In June 1965, having completed a full year in the Walker Brothers grocery business, Frank got word that he was eligible for a week's paid vacation. "Hearing this I immediately called my sister Marie in Truro. I asked her if she could put me up for a few days. When she agreed, I bought my ticket and headed for the London, Ontario, airport." He was heading home to catch up on what had happened in his old stomping grounds while he was away, and to share some stories of his own.

It is worth recalling that, in the 1960s, well before the days of the internet and social media, people far apart could stay in touch only by writing letters or making expensive long-distance phone calls. Frank MacKay had not written to his Lincoln bandmates in Truro while he was in Sarnia, nor had he spoken to any of them on the phone. He and they were living in their own separate worlds, nearly two thousand kilometres apart. The details of what Frank and the other Lincolns respectively had been up to over the past twelve months were unknown to each other.

News that Frank MacKay was back in town spread almost as fast as a lightning strike. As Frank put it, "I had no sooner stepped in Marie's front door when her phone began to ring nonstop. Each call was from a Lincoln member, welcoming me back to town and suggesting we get together."

Since Frank was going to be in Truro for only seven days, the getting together had to happen pretty quickly. That it did. And though the gatherings always began with remembrances of funny or outrageous events in The Lincolns's past, it was not long before the future came up. It seemed to all present that, although The Beatles and other British groups were still hugely popular, there was still room for the kind of music The Lincolns preferred to play, which was highly danceable R & B. In fact, the shared feeling was that the band should move more fully into that niche, separating itself from every other Maritime band. They could specialize in what the record industry was increasingly calling "soul."

Soul was a form of rhythm and blues with elements of gospel and jazz, a division of rock 'n' roll most often associated with artists who recorded on the Atlantic, Chess, Stax, and Motown labels. For the musicians based in Truro, it was a perfect fit. They all loved the music of Ray Charles, Otis Redding, and James Brown, along with that of Aretha Franklin, Sam Cooke, Wilson Pickett, and dozens of other Black American artists. Frank MacKay, if he would agree to come back to Truro, could interpret that material as though it was his birthright. As far as instruments went, they already had two horns in addition to the usual guitars and drums. They decided they should add an organ, too.

To top things off, a new venue was available: the Colchester Legion, on Truro's Brunswick Street. It had hosted radio station CKCL record hops in days gone by, dances that had drawn good-sized crowds. It could become the new home base for The Lincolns if they wanted it. There was no question that the Legion was a bigger and better venue than the old Pleasant Street Hall. If the band were to come back together and hold dances there, The Lincolns all agreed, they would attract even larger crowds than before.

All the optimistic talk about a glowing future back in Truro was enough to get the singer on vacation from Sarnia to make up his mind. He was all in. As Frank MacKay put it, looking back from late 2018, "the talk was all about putting the band back together. I had to admit it sounded pretty good to me. It was time to go home."

So, when Frank MacKay's week was up, he went back to Sarnia with his short-term future set. He now understood that there were uncertainties in the music business and always would be. It was the nature of the industry, based as it was on ever changing tastes. But what mattered most to Frank was that it meant being in the music business, a business he truly loved, and not working in a Sarnia grocery store! By moving to Ontario for a year he had shown that he could adapt when necessary. But for now—for the rest of 1965 and who knows how long after that—he was going to be a part of whatever the next phase of The Lincolns proved to be.

Frank gave two weeks' notice to both his grocery store job and his Sarnia band, and then returned to Truro, where he began practising once more with his old band. Only it wasn't exactly the same old band, as we will see in the next chapter.

But before we turn the page on The Lincolns's lull of 1964–65, let this chapter's closing words belong to Frank MacKay:

Looking back on my year in Ontario, I can now see that even at nineteen I was at a crossroads. Pursue music or leave it behind. To the city of Sarnia, my mother, sister, Walker Brothers, and all the fabulously kind folks who worked both stores, thanks for making the days I spent with you such a wonderful memory. Last but not least, a 'gigantic' shout out to Brian, Tim, Gary, and Ken, for inviting me to be a part of their young and energetic rock 'n' roll club. Thanks to you guys, I not only continued to follow the music, I followed my heart.

4

BETTER THAN EVER

1965–68

*A*fter *Frank MacKay's return to Truro in June 1965, he and the other* Lincolns set to work. The project was to breathe new life back into the band that had been dormant for thirteen months. They practised over the summer, usually at Rod Norrie's place. There, they figured out the songlist they would perform at the Legion in the fall. Some songs played from 1961 to 1963 stayed in; others were dropped, replaced by more recent R & B numbers. Frank MacKay's vote was decisive on whether a song was in or out, as the material had to fall into a style and vocal range with which he was comfortable. As before, lead guitarist Frank Mumford played a vital role in sorting out the song's key and the best arrangements for the instruments. In Frank MacKay's view, Frank Mumford was "the glue."

As befitting the shift that was underway, the group called itself The *New* Lincolns. It sounds funny now, because it recalls the many advertisements then on radio and TV for hundreds of products, each one boasting to be *new and improved*. Well, The Lincolns apparently felt the same—that they, too, were new and improved. Their fans, however, would rarely say the word "new" aloud. The band remained in popular parlance simply The Lincolns, no matter what it said on tickets and posters. That's also how I'll mostly refer to them in the remaining pages.

There was a practical reason for the small name change, one that was perhaps unspoken by the band but nonetheless likely important psychologically. That was to announce subtly to the world—and in particular to the musician they had dropped from the group—that this was not exactly the same old band. Gone from the group in 1965 was founding member and long-time bass player, the playful, unpredictable, free-spirited Brian Chisholm. Like Frank MacKay, Brian had moved away from Nova Scotia after the group broke up in 1964. Unlike Frank, Brian was not asked to come back to Truro to rejoin the band. Instead, The Lincolns thought they had found a new bass guitarist: sixteen-year-old Barry Ryan, who was playing lead guitar for another very popular Truro band, The Imperials. Frank MacKay gave him a call.

Though Barry admired The Lincolns and had been watching them play at the Pleasant Street Hall since he was thirteen, he said no. He had only recently become The Imperials's lead guitarist, moving over from bass, and didn't want to give up that role to play bass for The Lincolns. Instead, he recommended the band get in touch with a friend, another sixteen-year-old at Truro Senior High. That friend was Donnie Muir, who also happened to be the star quarterback of the town's football team. Of course, it wasn't Don's ball-handling skills The Lincolns were interested in, but his ability on guitar.

Don's journey to become a Lincoln in 1965 was anything but a straight line. His parents signed him up for piano lessons in 1956, when he was eight, but—like Rod Norrie with his violin lessons—Don "hated it so bad." His attitude to music changed only after he visited the house of family friend, Chalmers Doane, who had a basement full of every instrument imaginable. Doane

Don Muir playing bass with The Lincolns at the Truro Legion, 1966; with Peter Cox guesting at the mic and Frank MacKay on the Farfisa organ. Sax players Layne Francis and Lee Taylor were on a break. Once in a while, Don and Frank Mumford would trade instruments—for example, on "Walk That Walk," a 1965 hit for David Clayton Thomas and The Shays.
(PRIDHAM'S STUDIO)

was a leading figure in the teaching of music in Nova Scotia schools, and he encouraged young Don to try each and every instrument. It was an exploration Don remembers to this day. It taught him that music could be fun. When, at age ten, he received his own guitar for Christmas from his parents, he was delighted.

Not long after, however, Don was sent away—for three years and six days—to what was then the most prestigious private school in the province, King's Collegiate School in Windsor (today, King's-Edgehill School). He hated that life and called his mother on the sixth day of his fourth year, threatening to run away. Mrs. Muir brought Don home, where he entered Grade 9 at Truro Junior High. Back in Truro, he joined a band called The Calientes and liked practising at Barry Ryan's place, "jamming and showing each other chords and licks." Other members included Alex MacDougall and Morris Burris. Like the early days' Valiants/Lincolns, The Calientes played mostly instrumentals by groups like The Ventures but also a few songs with lyrics. Dick Brown sang with them sometimes, as did Judy Burns.

The musical highlight for Don Muir in 1963–64 was to see and hear The Lincolns play. They were, he recalled in 2018, "the first good live band I ever saw." He remembered standing alongside Barry Ryan many times near the roped-off stage at the Pleasant Street Hall, "drooling at the original band every Friday." The two aspiring musicians would study how the guys in The Lincolns performed. It was the same thing the guys in The Lincolns had once done with The Novatones. With Don and Barry, both wished in junior high that they could one day play with The Lincolns. As fate would have it, both did, with Don's dream coming true first.

Because he was still only in his mid-teens in 1963–64, Mrs. Muir, a local school teacher, insisted her son be home by eleven o'clock. Don complied, even when he went to see The Lincolns. He knew exactly how long it took him to run the 1.2 kilometres from the Pleasant Street Hall to his house at the far end of Smith Avenue, across from the golf course. His friend Barry Ryan's curfew was not until midnight, because Barry lived only half a block from the hall.

When Frank MacKay came back from Sarnia in June 1965 for a week's vacation—a week in which The Lincolns proposed they reform the band—Don Muir chanced to see Frank playing pickup baseball in the field behind Willow Street School. Seizing the opportunity, Don asked the singer if he would like to jam

Frank MacKay leads the Lincolns in a show at Dartmouth High School.

a bit. Frank was never one to miss a chance to express himself musically. "Sure," he said, and off they went to the Muir house, where there was a piano and guitars. (The house, incidentally, was two down from the Francis house, where saxophonist Layne grew up.) Don remembers the afternoon clearly, including Frank MacKay's singing the Tom Jones hit "It's Not Unusual" to Don's accompaniment.

The two musicians hit it off that afternoon, and in retrospect the encounter was an audition of sorts for young Don Muir. He more than passed the test. When Frank returned to Truro a few weeks later after bidding adieu to Sarnia, it was an easy fit to ask Don Muir to join the other band members out at the Norrie family farm when they started rehearsing as The New Lincolns.

IN LIVING COLOUR, 1966

In 1966, The New Lincolns hired Pridham's Studio to do a photo shoot, only this time they didn't want shots of themselves posing for the camera. Instead, they asked for photos and film footage of them doing what they did best: playing at a dance. Bob Pridham did what was asked. He took both colour film footage (without sound) and black and white still shots of the band performing at the Colchester Legion on a Friday night (from atop a ladder) and at the Pleasant Street Hall on a Saturday. The film footage is available on YouTube. The audio in both cases is of The Lincolns playing, but it comes from a later reunion. In a few spots, the audio and video seem to match, but at other times it is obvious there is no connection. Nevertheless, the two filmed sequences are the only known footage that captures what a genuine Lincolns dance was like in 1966. No one was jiving anymore—it was all the free-form style of the later sixties. Also on YouTube are other performances by The Lincolns at different reunions, including a nine-minute version from 2011 of "Dreams to Remember."

Don was thrilled of course, but also initially a little intimidated. He was just sixteen, while the others were mostly in their twenties. Moreover, the always serious Frank Mumford, the band's onstage conductor, would sometimes scowl at Don if he hit a sour note. Lee Taylor, closest in age to Don, became his "best friend in the band."

If there had been any uncertainty as to whether or not Truro would welcome the return of The Lincolns, all such doubt disappeared when hundreds of fans showed up at Legion Branch 26 one Friday night in the fall of 1965 for the first Lincolns dance in over a year. The band's long absence made people appreciate them all the more. Unlike in 1964, when dancers were demanding Beatles songs, the audience now wanted exactly what The Lincolns were dishing out: their adaptations of the great soul hits of the day.

Before we explore in more detail how the people down on the dance floors of the Maritimes felt about the band up onstage, I think it best to introduce John Gray, who was asked to become the seventh member of The Lincolns in the spring of 1966.

John Howard Gray was born in Ottawa in 1946 but moved with his parents to Truro at a young age. (Decades later, when he became a novelist, John renamed himself John MacLachlan Gray to distinguish himself from another novel-writing John Gray.) The Gray parents urged their kids to learn to play a musical instrument. The three boys—John, Charles, and Philip—did, and each went on to play professionally. Sister Karen, in John's view, "didn't get the same level of encouragement."

Contacted in the fall of 2018, John confessed to having been "a terrible student, in and out of school. Today I would be diagnosed with ADD and fed Ritalin until I couldn't blink both eyes at the same time. My low boredom threshold meant that I didn't 'pay attention' in class, and I didn't practise the piano. But I did *play* the piano—a lot by ear; everything from jazz to The Beatles. It was a kind of refuge."

John Gray on the Hammond organ.
(JOHN MACLACHLAN GRAY)

Thinking back to the stories of all the other Lincolns, it's likely that music was a refuge for each of them as well. The band itself was a refuge: an activity and a small group of friends who shared a common passion.

John Gray's musical passion began with piano teacher Harold Berino, a post–Second World War refugee to Canada who was the organist at Truro's Presbyterian church. In Europe, he had survived first Hitler and then Stalin. As John remembered it, Mr. Berino "despaired of my progress—I *never* practised—until it came time to compete in the music festival where I would win. In the end he just let me play pieces I liked—Beethoven, Rachmaninoff—and seemed pleased with the result. Once he said that a piece I played was 'good music.' Big compliment, that. The problem was, I never learned to read music. Mr. Berino would play the piece for me, and from then on I would pick it out by ear and use the written music as a sort of general guide—were the notes going up or down? That sort of thing. I don't think he ever realized I could hardly sight-read a note."

It paints quite a picture: an accomplished, Old World traditionalist music teacher hoodwinked by a musically talented precocious kid who only pretends to read the sheet music when in fact he is actually remembering in his head how the notes are supposed to go. Unsurprisingly, the gifted John Gray could easily play rock 'n' roll by ear.

As a teenager in Truro, John eventually came to know Layne Francis, who, John said, "was the only person I had met who was interested in jazz." That friendship led occasionally to John's "sitting in" with The Lincolns on trumpet—not as a member of the band but as guest soloist. After all, not many numbers on their songlist called for a trumpet. John also "played trumpet with the Imperials, but on fewer and fewer songs." John recounted that, when he headed off to Mount Allison University in the fall of 1964, "I expect the Imperials were glad to be rid of me."

John Gray was at Mount A for the next two years but often got together with Layne Francis whenever he was back in Truro. The two would "listen to jazz and drive around in his red convertible with a 390 hp engine." Then, in the spring of 1966, after John completed what he describes as "a mediocre year" at Mount A, a fresh opportunity to play with The Lincolns presented itself. As John remembered it, Frank MacKay had bought "a Farfisa organ and found it was pretty hard to concentrate on playing and singing" at the same time. Frank asked John if he'd like to buy the organ and join the band. John did both at one fell swoop. In that way, The Lincolns became a seven-man band. Once again, the only important measuring stick was the quality of the sound. As always, The Lincolns wanted it to be as big, bold, and soulful as possible. Frank MacKay made that abundantly clear at one

John Gray playing the Hammond organ.
(JOHN MACLACHLAN GRAY)

school dance. John recalled: "After two requests for songs by the Monkees, Frank announced that The Lincolns were never coming back. Ever."

Around this time the band came up with a slogan for the musical experience they were offering. It was a good one, and so very apt: "Join in the Soul." Sherry O'Brien-Stevens affirmed that the band's tag line for late 1960s came from Layne Francis and reflected the strong influence of the Island, the Black community where The Lincolns often went to Murray Dorrington's to drink and jam. The poster image of a clapping Frank MacKay was developed by Tim Forbes, then a student at Dartmouth High who went on to become an acclaimed artist in Toronto.

The image and slogan of The Lincolns, late 1960s; the poster was developed by Dartmouth High student Tim Forbes, later a graphic artist and visual artist in Toronto. (DESIGN BY TIM FORBES)

In April 2019, Forbes responded to my inquiry as to how that poster came to be. He began by describing Frank MacKay "as the big voice of The Lincolns. He was the soul sound of a generation. My friends and I would regularly drive fifty-five

The photograph upon which the "Join in the Soul" poster was based; visible behind a clapping Frank MacKay is Don Muir on bass, playing what Barry Ryan identified as a Gibson EB-0.
(DOUG HILTZ/ JANE BAILEY)

miles from Dartmouth to the Truro Legion just to hear The Lincolns." One of the tasks Tim Forbes took on while at Dartmouth High was to create handmade posters for different bands that played at the school. "Somewhere along the line, I got my hands on a stage photo of Frank. Based on that, I drew the graphic Frank image with a rapidograph pen, with hand lettering done for a poster."

Tim remembered taking the poster art backstage to show Layne Francis and Frank MacKay at the Legion. "When Frank saw it, he boomed in his drawn-out baritone: '*Bah-yutee-full.*' That was gold—the ultimate seal of approval."

With that green light, Tim took his poster design to a commercial printer, Bromoc Print in Dartmouth. It was the first time he had ever done that—and so began what would be an extremely successful career in graphic design for Forbes. He would later move to Toronto and eventually transition into a visual artist as a sculptor, photographer, and painter. Yet, notwithstanding his many successes, Tim Forbes retains a special affection for the poster he created for the 1960s Truro band. In his own words, "Today, a copy of The New Lincolns's 'Join in the Soul' poster is a part of an archive (The Tim Forbes Special Collection) established in 2015 by the TIFF Resource Library—documenting my studio's work for Canada's performing arts, cultural events, musicians, and film and television productions. Of the myriad of works I have produced over the years, 'Join in the Soul' remains my favourite. It encapsulates a genesis, a generation of friends, and the music that never dies."

The iconic image of Frank MacKay clapping that Tim Forbes used in the poster image was based on a photo taken by another Dartmouth High student, Doug Hiltz. The photo was included as a full-page image in the *Spectator*, the Dartmouth High yearbook, for 1968 and captures the essence of the power and energy of the new version of The Lincolns.

The Farfisa organ that John Gray took over in 1966 was a relatively new addition to the arsenal of rock 'n' roll instruments. Sam the Sham and the Pharaohs' 1965 hit "Woolly Bully" was one of the first records to feature the Farfisa sound. In 1966, that organ was also featured on Percy Sledge's monster hit, "When a Man Loves a Woman." Clearly, a Farfisa was a decent instrument

THE HAMMOND

While the Farfisa was an effective organ for a rock 'n' roll band, being relatively small and easily moved around, the Hammond was in a completely different league. It had a wonderfully powerful sound but was far bigger and much heavier than a Farfisa. It could not easily be taken on the road. Nonetheless, the priority for The Lincolns was always the quality and power of the sound. One day in 1966, Frank Mumford came into the weekly practice at the Legion with the day's *Halifax Chronicle Herald*. "There's a Hammond for sale," he said, "with a tone cabinet and revolving speakers. Two thousand dollars. We should go get it." The other Lincolns agreed.

First, however, they needed to be sure they could meet the asking price. Down to Smith Avenue the band went, to talk to the manager of the local Bank of Nova Scotia branch. They found him not at home but on the nearby golf course. The moment he stepped off the green at the ninth hole, The Lincolns pressed him for a loan. The manager's reply came with a laugh: "Christ, you guys are all rich. You've all got new cars. Yes, I'll lend you the money."

With their truck, the band headed to Tantallon to purchase the Hammond with its tone cabinet from a Dalhousie University professor, athletic director Ken Gowie. Immediately after, they proceeded to Buckley's music store in Halifax, where, for a couple hundred more, they traded the Hammond tone cabinet for a superior Leslie cabinet.

The new Hammond—a C3 model that weighed two hundred kilograms—gave the band the sound it sought. Yet it also meant some very heavy and tricky lifting when they took it on the road. In Rod Norrie's words: "We took it up steps and into back alleys God only knows. It went into places where you couldn't get the damn thing. But we always got it in, one way or another."

The Lincolns could use until a better organ—a Hammond—became available not long after John Gray joined the band.

The two newest Lincolns, Don Muir and John Gray, each found the process by which songs were added to band's repertoire to be intriguing. Don recalled that the songlist was a mix of rhythm and blues, old rock 'n' roll, and a bit of blues. Every Sunday afternoon the band would get together at the Legion to rehearse, with five or six new songs considered. It was almost always Frank MacKay who brought in material he had heard somewhere—usually on the radio—that he thought would be a good fit. One exception was when Rod Norrie brought in a cassette tape of the great Eddie Floyd number "Knock on Wood," which he had heard in a nightclub in Bermuda. The band agreed it was a terrific song and found the 45 in a Truro record store. Looking back on the selection process, Frank MacKay admitted a few of his choices "were out in left field"—like "Tar and Cement"—but the other guys in the band went along with them for a few weeks. Of the five or six new songs considered in a typical week, Don Muir recalls, four new ones would be worked up for the next dance.

It sounds pretty simple. John Gray, however, who came on board nearly a year after Don, saw the process as a little more complicated. Or chaotic. In his book, *Local Boy Makes Good*, John writes of how, at rehearsals, the band would put a new 45 on the turntable, and everyone would try to learn their respective parts "all at once." No one, in John Gray's recollection, had "the patience to listen to the song from beginning to end before attempting to play it." The key figure in the learning process was lead guitarist Frank Mumford, who, Gray wrote in a late 2018 email, "basically directed the band in performance. Mumford was the platoon sergeant, keeping our shit together." Twenty years earlier, in *Local Boy Makes Good*, John had written: "We flailed away at it for an hour until it began to take some sort of shape, and cleaned up the rough edges in performance. Inadvertently, The Lincolns had their own unique sound. Is that creativity? Or were we just a bad copy of someone else?"

I vote for creativity. That's because The Lincolns's versions were pretty much always as good as—and often better than—whatever was on the original vinyl. Moreover, because the songs were played live for a large crowd of dancers, not recorded in a studio for play on the radio, the band could extend each song however it wanted, with several of the musicians up on the stage getting a chance to have long solos not found in the originals. A two-minute song routinely became six, eight, or ten minutes long, the dancers lapping up every extra second.

And speaking of those living, breathing fans, they loved that first performance by The New Lincolns in the fall of 1965 and came back in growing numbers every Friday night thereafter over the next four years. Whatever limit the fire marshal placed on the Truro Legion, many nights that number was utterly ignored. In 1968 and 1969, crowds of a thousand became routine. On a few occasions—typically during university Christmas breaks, when all the Truro-area college kids were back in town—the number of paying customers went higher still. Rod Norrie recalls one night watching the money count hit 1,142. Frank MacKay was told that another night it was 1,300. Those are pretty big numbers: ten per cent of the population in a town of 12,000.

So firm was The Lincolns's grasp on the musical tastes of the Truro area that touring musicians learned not to even try to compete. If there was a Lincolns dance going on anywhere—at the Legion on a Friday night or at the Truro Golf Club, North River's Red Barn, or at the Pleasant Street Hall on a Saturday night—that's where people would go. Don Muir recalled hearing that visiting artists sometimes sold only a handful of tickets if

The Lincolns were playing nearby. When Bobby Curtola came to town to play at the Colchester Stadium, his manager hired The Lincolns as the opening act to ensure that his artist would get a crowd.

The local radio station tapped into The Lincolns's massive popularity by hiring them to come up with a theme song for the hit parade time slot of deejay Graham Wylie. The band took the mostly instrumental tune "Watermelon Man," written by Herbie Hancock and released in 1963 by Mongo Santamaria, and gave it lyrics, "The Graham Wylie Show." The bit was recorded at the Legion, the band setting up on the floor, not onstage.

The band was, of course, delighted by the crowds at the Legion and elsewhere. They could see from the stage that there were hundreds more than they had played for back in the early days. Indeed, with standing-room-only situations, it was a challenge for dancers to find enough space to move about.

Appreciative crowds also greeted The Lincolns and their songlist wherever they played around the Maritimes. Typically, that was at high schools or on college campuses. More about those road trips in the next chapter, but it is important to note here that a fair number of fans who saw The Lincolns play in other towns often made the trek to Truro to see the band play at home, which drove up the Truro crowds. Dr. Scott Murray, a Halifax dermatologist who grew up in Pictou, recalled that, "because of The Lincolns, Truro was our New York." Bridgewater's David R. Hubley, later a judge in Truro, felt the same way. He and his friends heard a lot of talk about The Lincolns in their South Shore town, about how you had to get to Truro to experience them. So they did. Fridays, he and his friends would travel an hour and a half each way from Bridgewater, sometimes sleeping overnight in their Volkswagen. Later, David Hubley would enjoy The Lincolns over and over again as a student at Mount

PUNCHING THE COLONEL'S WIFE

From time to time, members of The Lincolns played gigs as independent musicians, without the rest of the band. Rod Norrie recalls that one night he played drums and Layne Francis played sax for piano player Freddie Cormier. It was a formal military affair at the Armouries on Willow Street in Truro. Frank MacKay and Lee Taylor showed up late in the evening for the fun of it, offering to sing and play a second sax without being paid. Neither was in formal attire, which offended some of those in attendance. But once Frank sang a song, everyone applauded and asked for more. Lee, however, of small stature and dressed casually, was shown a complete cold shoulder. Worse than that, he was pushed from behind and went tumbling down two steps.

Rod was incensed to see his friend mistreated, especially when Lee had volunteered to play for nothing. Rod asked Freddie Cormier to speak up for Lee, but Freddie did not. He relied on gigs at the Armouries and didn't want to ruffle any feathers. At the end of the night, with his drum kit packed up and over his shoulder, Rod made sure he had words with those he felt had mistreated Lee Taylor.

First up was a manager from the Bank of Montreal, who told Rod: "You take your drums and get the hell out of here."

Rod whacked the cigarette dangling from the bank manager's lips, but did not hit his face. In response, the colonel's wife grabbed Rod's tie, sliding its knot as tight as she could against his throat. Starting to choke, Rod reacted instinctively. "I tagged her and down she went to the floor. I looked up and there was the colonel, who took a swing at me. I ducked and countered with a punch that flattened his nose. Everybody was screaming and yelling."

An instant later, three big sergeants in kilts were standing before Rod. "Sir, you'd better take your drums and leave," one sergeant said. Rod replied: "You hear that noise? That's me leaving."

But when the sergeants got Rod down a flight of stairs, away from the commotion, The Lincolns's drummer was surprised to hear: "The sergeants would like to buy you a drink in the sergeants' mess." Apparently, Rod was an instant hero for standing up to an unpopular and officious colonel and his wife. "They loved me," Rod recalled.

Allison. In Judge Hubley's words, composed in 2019, the Truro band was "the perfect rock and roll storm."

Another fan of the band was Gary Ramey, who grew up in tiny Crousetown, in Lunenburg County. While attending Mount Allison between 1966 and 1969, Gary couldn't get enough of The Lincolns. Looking back on those years from the vantage point of 2018, Gary affirmed that the band's performances were "my happiest recollections of my time at Mount A. First, The Lincolns played in the old gym, then in Beethoven Hall." It seemed to him as though the Truro band played on campus every Saturday night, because he could not remember any other band ever playing there. Of course, that wasn't the case, but Rod Norrie did offer that the band loved playing at Mount A: "It was a favourite place to play." Gary Ramey went on to become a teacher and musician, earn a PhD, and later serve as an MLA in the Nova Scotia legislature from 2009 to 2013. Thinking back to his time at Mount Allison, he affirmed that everyone on campus "loved The Lincolns and thought them the best band they had ever heard." Gary also recalled that, on Saturday afternoons prior to a Lincolns dance, everyone on campus could be seen carrying athletic bags. It wasn't sports equipment inside the bags—it was booze. Alcohol was not allowed on campus, so the students had to hide their beer or spirits.

Patricia Starratt (then Patty Ross) was a Kentville fan. She and a friend first caught the band at a dance at King's Collegiate School in Windsor when she was fifteen. Both were hooked immediately, especially by the twin saxes of Layne Francis and Lee Taylor. Whenever the band played anywhere in the area, they made sure to be there. They even hitchhiked to Truro one snowy winter's night to see The Lincolns at the Legion. They were not disappointed. Fifty years later, walking around the track at the Canada Games Centre in Halifax and talking to this author, Starratt sang the praises of The Lincolns: "They knocked me over with the big sound. They were unlike any other band I'd ever heard."

Fans in Truro, of course, were the lucky ones who heard The Lincolns the most. That could be fifty-two times a year if they wished. Although the core band was set, from time to time The Lincolns welcomed guests up onstage. One was Bruce Jackson,

This 1966 dance at the Pleasant Street Hall was one of the last held there; by then, the Truro Legion had become the band's new base.

who did James Brown–inspired routines that everyone loved. Another was Peter Cox; he specialized in songs by Eric Burdon and The Animals. Bubs Brown, a renowned guitarist from the Annapolis Valley, also played with The Lincolns for a spell. He would come up to Truro on the train, in time for the Friday night Legion dance. Giving other musicians a chance to show what they could do was an important part of the Lincolns experience. The fans loved it.

One Truro fan in the late 1960s was Maxine Wallace. She recalled in 2018: "I remember the genuine love we felt for their music. I always joked (although the sentiment behind the joke was real) that if The Beatles played across the street on Friday night, no one would go." And further: "It was a great feeling when Friday rolled around. You never asked people if they were going [to the Lincolns dance] that night because you knew they were. It took something major to keep someone away."

In a subsequent email, Maxine asked me if I shared another happy memory of hers: "Do you remember when the saxes would blast out those first three guttural notes of 'Knock on Wood'? I can still hear them clearly in my head. They triggered a wild rush to the dance floor every time."

I do recall that, and it was great. I think the opening notes of "Mustang Sally," "Land Of A Thousand Dances," and "In the Midnight Hour" generated similar reactions. A different response entirely—but one of equally rapt attention from the dance floor—came when the crowd heard the beginning of "Danny Boy." The early twentieth-century ballad about the absence and loss of a loved one, set to a much older Irish tune, might seem like an unusual choice for a soul and R & B band. But Frank MacKay loved the melancholy air and sang it with both tenderness and power. It was as though he was expressing his innermost self, which he likely was, as you will see when you read this book's Afterword. "Danny Boy" quickly became the standard slow dance at nearly every Lincolns event. Some danced, but many more in the crowd simply stood and admired the vocal range of Frank MacKay. Two other immensely popular slow dance songs were "Cry to Me" and "When Something is Wrong With My Baby." Frank belted them out as though he was living through the heartbreak every time.

Maxine Wallace's only sour memory was of "how the dance floor [at the Legion] was segregated into sections. Everyone knew exactly where the lines were and which section was theirs." Joy O'Brien also remembered the separation of the dance floor into different groups: "I was such a square peg in high school—I was never any part of any 'in' crowd. I loved going to the Lincolns dances, although I was never sure which section I was supposed to stand in!" Joy also recalled the advice she once received: "If you're cool, you wait until first intermission to go in. If you're really cool, you wait for second intermission." Joy says: "I could never wait."

Long-time Lincolns fan Danny Joseph suggested the dance floor at the Legion was "a tapestry," with the West End and East End kids in their separate areas, and distinct again were those from Millbrook, Salmon River, Belmont, the Black community, and so on. Fifty years on, Colin Topshee could clearly picture that dance floor. It included a few individuals who stood out most weeks, like "The Lone Twister" and "The Lone Twister's Sister," a sibling duo the crowd liked to urge on, more in mockery than in admiration.

My own take on the separation of groups at the Friday night Legion dances is that it was a division by networks of friends, places of origin, and some unwritten "coolness" index. The entire right-hand side of the floor was—from the perspective of my friends at the time—where the kids from rural Colchester County went. Snobs that we were, we smiled at some of their choices in haircuts, clothes, and footwear. As if we from Truro were wearing designer outfits from Paris and Milan! The truth was that we were wearing bell-bottom jeans and button-down Oxford cloth shirts from Margolians just like the county kids. In any case, my friends and I always planted our feet somewhere on the left side of the hall, from the midpoint of the room to the back. Those everyone deemed to be the coolest kids—either by the styles they wore or by whom they were friends with, like The Lincolns themselves—were always about halfway toward the front on the left. The Black kids mostly danced at the very front, close to the stage. I did not see that as any kind of segregation, nor do I now. Rather, I think they were choosing to be where the live music and the musicians playing it moved them the most.

A highlight of most dances was when Frank MacKay would come down off the stage and swing through the adoring crowd—

with Layne Francis playing his mellow sax on his shoulders. Lee Taylor weighed half what Layne did, but no matter—it was usually Layne aloft for this part of the night. When asked where that practice came from, Frank shrugged: "I don't know. Somewhere." Less often, but equally crowd pleasing, was when Frank would lie on the floor and writhe with delight to have Layne and Lee playing their respective saxes into each ear. In 2018, I asked Frank if he ever wore ear plugs to protect his hearing during that stunt, or at any other time. "What?" he said cupping his ear with a big grin. "I've got some hearing problems," he admitted. How could he not?

None of The Lincolns, in fact, ever gave eventual hearing loss—a reality they all suffer from—the slightest thought back in the day. It was a microcosm of the dominant spirit of the 1960s: everyone under thirty seemed to believe they were going to be eternally young!

Some in the crowd looked at The Lincolns as if they were The Beatles. By that I mean they each picked their favourites, as many did with John, Paul, George, and Ringo. Karen MacLean told me in 2019 that Frank Mumford was "the pretty boy of the group." The lead guitarist certainly seemed to be the one with the most girlfriends. I spoke with three while writing this book, and heard from another woman that Mumford had "a roving eye." For Helen Dorrington-Price, organist John Gray was the favourite. She told me her friends each had theirs—among Rod, Don, Frank, Frank, Layne, and Lee. For two Kentville girls, so I heard in 2018, their favourite was Lee Taylor, the one closest in size to them.

One of the greatest Lincolns fans was my best friend, Craig Stanfield. I loved the band's music and high-energy performances, but Craig.... Well, Craig's affection went beyond love. When we went off together to Dalhousie University in the fall of 1968,

The Lincolns in 1966, playing an instrumental to give hard-working singer Frank MacKay a short break.
(PRIDHAM'S STUDIO)

sharing a room in the Howe Hall residence, I sometimes stayed in Halifax on the weekend to see what the city had to offer. Craig, however, rarely stayed away from Truro. He had a girl-friend in the Hub Town at least part of that time, but it was mainly because he didn't want to miss The Lincolns. In Craig's own words: "I was one of the faithful contingent of Truro and Colchester County boys who returned home from university, often by way of hitchhiking, almost every weekend. The only weekends I can remember staying in Halifax were those when they [The Lincolns] were playing at Dal or SMU [Saint Mary's University]. I also recall travelling to other locales where they played, such as New Glasgow."

Though not seen in this 1967 photo taken at the Nova Scotia Provincial Exhibition, Rod Norrie is off to the right, keeping the beat going for singer Frank MacKay. Left to right: Lee Taylor, Layne Francis, Frank Mumford, Frank MacKay, and Don Muir.
(COURTESY OF LAYNE FRANCIS)

Craig credits Maxine Wallace as the one who introduced him in 1966 to the Friday night Lincolns dances. "I was hooked (and grateful to this day that she did)." For her part, Maxine cherishes her memory of how much Craig loved Frank MacKay up onstage. "I can visualize Craig perfectly, his head tilted slightly to the side, listening, the joy in the laugh that would slip out when it just got to be too much for him to hold inside."

Just how important were those dances to Craig? Well, he confesses, "If I was given a 'Back to the Future' opportunity to go back in time for one day/partial day and, in no way trying to be disrespectful to my wife Joanne and my family and all the great things/memories I have, it would be Friday at the Legion in the summer of, say, 1968, when I believe The Lincolns were in their prime."

Frank MacKay had a way of mesmerizing the crowd when he sang. (DALHOUSIE UNIVERSITY ARCHIVES)

I suspect Craig is not the only one with such a wish. In fact, there is proof. Whenever a Lincolns Reunion comes around—which they have several times since the first in 1978—the tickets are snapped up and waiting lists created. Those reunion concerts are a form of time travel, I have to think. Attendees get their most cherished band back up onstage, and they themselves feel like they're seventeen again! It's the closest we mortals get to going back in time.

As much fun as the reunion dances are, the original Lincolns dances of the 1960s were substantially different affairs. The music is a constant, more or less, but much else is changed. And I'm not talking about clothing and hairstyles, though they are definitely not the same.

In the 1960s, no tables and chairs took up valuable space on any dance floor. Everyone was in their teens or early twenties—not

Frank MacKay having fun during the 1978 reunion.
(COURTESY OF ELEANOR AND ROD NORRIE)

their sixties or seventies—and no one needed or wanted anywhere to sit. At the Legion, instead of three or four hundred, back then sometimes more than a thousand people squeezed in to fight for space to dance, stand, or mill about. In the sixties, no bar legally sold alcohol to anyone under nineteen. For those seeking intoxication—and there were more than a few—beverages were consumed on the sly outside, maybe in a car in the parking lot. Danny Joseph told me in December 2018 that he and his four closest friends began their preparations for the weekly Lincolns dance as soon as school was out by consuming Ten Penny ales.

From my perspective, the biggest difference between The Lincolns's dances then and now is that the ones in the 1960s had not the slightest hint of nostalgia. They were unscripted dramas that everyone came to observe and maybe play a role in. What I mean is that, back then, most of the people at the dances were single, so there was always an air of the hunt on the dance floor. Maybe "hunt" is too strong a term. Primal longings? Still too much. Let's just say there was an air of possible romance—and by air, I mean pheromones. For the young men and women who came to Lincolns dances, in Truro or elsewhere, did not just show up to listen to the band; they also came to keep an eye on, and maybe dance with, someone in whom they were interested. If they were lucky, they would dance together. And luckier still, maybe walk home together. And then...well, let's just leave it at that. And no matter what happened on any particular Friday night, there'd be another one in seven days, where and when we would all get to do it over again.

What was so wonderful about the weekly dramas at the Legion was that they unfolded with this incredible soundtrack provided by The Lincolns. The greatest soul and R & B numbers from the 1960s did not just move our feet; they spoke to our deepest longings and setbacks. Teenagers that we were, we were not always able to express our feelings. Maybe that should read: we were *rarely* or *never* able to express our feelings. But, backed by a tight band, with horns blaring and organ rising, Frank MacKay sang for each and all of us. For those who never heard Frank, he was something like Joe Cocker, before anyone (in North America, at least) had ever heard of Joe Cocker. His powerful voice could reflect Ray Charles, Otis Redding, Wilson Pickett, and many other soul singers. With some songs, Frank celebrated the exultation of love; with others, it was the pain of a broken heart. Either way, Frank MacKay expressed what we were feeling on any given night, depending on how our individual love-life dramas were unfolding at the time. In short, The Lincolns's songlist infused and confirmed every possible mood down on the floor. It was powerful and irresistible and why so many of us have The Lincolns and their music embedded in our hearts, brains, and souls.

But it wasn't all peace and love at Lincolns dances. I can't provide reliable statistics on how many fights there were, but they were certainly not uncommon. My guess is that there were one or two a night, usually on the right-hand side of the dance floor. Danny Joseph, who was typically on that side, agreed. He recalled that he and his friends regularly got into fights with kids from Belmont. Why? Danny shook his head: "It's just the way it was." And then Danny added that he and a friend were once at a Lincolns dance in New Glasgow when an eye-opening fight occurred. In that melee, a piano on an upper floor was pushed through a picture window, crashing down a dozen feet to the ground.

Rod Norrie laughed when I asked him about fights, and proceeded to tell me about the night two guys started slugging it out up close to the stage. One of the cops up in that area, the very strong Albert Jackson, quickly intervened. "He picked up each one by the scruff of his neck, kicked the nearby emergency door open, and tossed them both outside." And that was that.

Occasionally there were moments of anger among The Lincolns themselves. Rod recalled the time one of his bandmates took exception to some teasing when the money was being divvied up in the back room at the Legion at the end of the night. At the joking suggestion that he might be taking more than his share, the guy in question hurled his beer bottle at the brick wall. Brew and shards of glass went everywhere. "I quit," he said. That flash of temper soon passed, and all was well again.

From time to time, there were fights on the left-hand side of the Legion dance floor. Mary Topshee recalls one when she was seated atop the radiators against the wall. Out of the blue, two guys started swinging away at each other beside her feet. Mary lifted hers knees up as high as she could so as not to get struck by any blows. Mary also remembers how she set aside a bit of money each week from her after-school $1.15 an hour job at Sanderson's cornerstore—so she could buy something nice at Reitmans to wear to a Friday night Lincolns dance.

One Friday, I even had a scuffle of my own. I was standing by Maxine Wallace, my girlfriend at the time, when this tall, skinny guy with a scowl on his face came along, wobbling slightly as he lurched toward the two of us. I'll call him Dean—because that was, in fact, his real name. Well, Dean reached out to touch Maxine in a way I didn't like, so I pushed him. A split second later, we were trading wildly swinging blows. My friends quickly pulled us apart, and it was over just like that—no need for the cops to intervene. Maxine's memory matches mine: "It only lasted a minute or so, but it was so shocking it felt as if the earth had slipped off its axis." That was because, to put it mildly, fighting was not my thing. Though, for the record, I once received a strap across the hands in Grade 4 or 5 at Willow Street School because I had been involved in a schoolyard tussle.

As Dean headed away from us, I recall Maxine's saying, close to my ear, "That wasn't really about me at all. That was two male egos." Or something like that. Her comment made me blink. In any case, Maxine aptly summarizes what happened next: "I remember we went outside and sat on the steps. I think we were both in a bit of a daze, trying to process what had happened. Then the door opened and Mike Saxton shuffled past, tossing over his shoulder, 'Sayin', Rocky?' That cracked us up, and the world righted itself."

That was my one and only fight at a Lincolns dance, and so far, the last one in my life. I'm hoping to keep it that way.

And that's likely enough about the good old Legion dances. Let's shift our focus away from Truro and go out on the road with the band.

5
ON THE ROAD
1965–68

From the fall of 1965 onward, road trips were a weekly fact of life for The Lincolns. Friday nights were reserved for dances at the Legion in Truro, but Saturday nights always found them playing somewhere else, and sometimes on Sundays, too. Back then, there were no divided highways anywhere in the Maritimes, only slow, winding, crooked stretches on nearly every road. That meant trips took much longer than they do today. Yet, incredibly, The Lincolns rarely stayed overnight. They would pack up after the show ended at midnight or one o'clock, then drive back to Truro, where they would arrive in the early hours of the morning.

Most travel was within a two-hundred-kilometre radius of Truro. For example, the band often travelled to Sackville, New Brunswick, to play at Mount Allison University, or to Halifax and Dartmouth or to the Annapolis Valley or Antigonish. But there were longer trips, to Saint John and Fredericton, and even to Sydney, on Cape Breton Island—in those days, a four- or five-hour drive. The Lincolns would leave Truro around noon, and start back about 1:00 A.M. after packing everything up, getting back to Truro as the sun was coming up. Later, with roadies to look after the equipment, the trip was shorter by an hour at each end. Jack Lilly, who became the band's drummer in 1968, remembers sleeping as best he could on the flat area above the back seat and beneath the rear window. This was long before there was any seat belt legislation.

The Lincolns were a huge hit in Sydney, where they usually played in the gym at Sydney Academy. One of the kids in the high school crowd in the mid-1960s was Sam Moon, who would go on to become a legendary Nova Scotia rock 'n' roller of his own. At the time, Sam was, in his words, "just starting in the local garage jamming scene." When he and his friends checked out The Lincolns at an Academy dance for the first time, they were stunned. Sam recalls: "It was like a huge freight train roaring down the track. Syncopated grooves, roaring solos, pumping bass. Sweet soul. Then this voice bigger than the room soaring high above. Frank MacKay shaking the earth! We knew we had a lot of work to do, the bar was set pretty high."

Another recollection of those Sydney Academy dances comes from Barry Ryan, who started playing bass guitar with The Lincolns in 1968. The first time he played at the Academy, he was told there was a record-breaking crowd of 2,300 in attendance, which was double the usual number that squeezed into Truro's Legion. Barry remembered: "So we walk onstage and the crowd goes nuts. Twenty-three hundred! It was just packed." In addition to the size of the audience, Barry couldn't get over how the Academy dance worked: "The girls are in the centre and all the guys walk around. Big circle, like a racetrack."

"Like sharks?" I suggested.

"Exactly," Barry said. "Eventually the guys ask the girls to dance, and they dance in the centre of all the girls. It was the weirdest thing. I'd never seen anything like it." And that says something, because Barry and The Lincolns played a lot of dances.

Another area where The Lincolns played a lot was Pictou County. It was at a high school dance in New Glasgow that a young Wayne Nicholson—later to become a renowned rock singer on the Maritimes music scene—first experienced the Truro band. In Wayne's own words: "In the mid- to late sixties, you couldn't help but hear about The Lincolns. They were said to be the best band in the Maritimes. When I first saw them at my high school, I saw and heard why. They were simply better than all the other groups of the day. Their playing and their presence: they knocked you out. One of the reasons I think was because they stuck to R & B and soul.... Having the incredible voice and stage presence of Frank MacKay certainly didn't hurt. He was one of the greatest R & B soul singers with built-in feeling this country has ever produced."

Regardless of The Lincolns's destination, until mid-1968 it generally worked out that Rod Norrie drove one car and Layne Francis the other, and each was their personal vehicle. The band sometimes reimbursed some of the gas money but rarely the full amount. That would become a sore point later on, when Frank Mumford wanted compensation for coming up from Halifax to rehearse or play in Truro. Rod and Layne felt they had been subsidizing the band for years by absorbing some of the cost of those trips. That was beside the point from Frank Mumford's perspective. He wanted gas money. The issue led to a cooling of what had long been a deep friendship between Rod Norrie and Frank Mumford.

In Barry Ryan's recollection of his first trip to and from Sydney, he travelled in Frank Mumford's car along with Frank MacKay and Donnie Muir. All the way home, Mumford's right hand would go up and someone would put an opened beer bottle in it. Sometime later, after he had polished it off, Mumford would lower his driver's side window, transfer the bottle to his

SETTING UP AND TAKING DOWN

As the size of the band grew, so did the number and sizes of the various instruments—speakers, drums, guitars, saxes, Hammond organ and tone cabinet. Out of necessity, The Lincolns had to start using a truck. Rod Norrie first bought a 1963 Chevy half-ton, and then a newer Ford, for which he built a special box to keep the equipment safe and dry. Later on, starting in 1968, after Rod had left the band, The Lincolns hired roadies: James "Lukey" Maxwell and Scott "Dinkles" Clyke to begin with, and later Frank Borden, too.

Those equipment guys would leave Truro well before the band, taking everything with them and setting up at the venue all ready to play. Lukey Maxwell recalled that the heavy Hammond was by far "the biggest obstacle, and man, we had to go up a lot of steps with that thing, and you needed three or four guys to lift it." Once they had everything set up, Lukey said he'd often mutter aloud: "Are the boys going to show up?" They always did. Remembering that era, Lukey said: "It was a lot of fun. The boys didn't worry about anything. They'd play, then leave the stage, and we'd clear everything. The boys loved it." The breakdown took an hour or two, depending on the location. Then, just like the musicians, the roadies would head back to Truro, where they would arrive early the next morning.

Once in a while, Frank MacKay played a little sax alongside Layne Francis after the latter had showed him how to produce a note or two.
(COURTESY OF LAYNE FRANCIS)

left hand, and throw the empty over the top of the car into the woods. And then his right arm would go up looking for another one. The car and its passengers made it home safely.

Considering how many road trips the band made, inevitably there would be mishaps and misadventures. How could there not be, considering the old, narrow Maritime roads they were driving on? And factoring in how exhausted and exhilarated the band would be after a three-hour, high-energy performance? With more than a little alcohol running through their veins?

From today's perspective, driving when tired and intoxicated is a high-risk practice that is beyond foolish. It's deadly dangerous. But we are talking about a much different era, long before MADD came into existence and the police introduced Breathalyzer tests. Back in the days when the young guys who were The Lincolns were coming of age, there was rarely a murmur that drinking and driving might be bad. A road trip for young males routinely meant taking along lots of beer; it was how it was. Yes, each year saw deadly accidents that killed young adult males, but at the time people seemed to think that was how it had to be. Add in that these particular guys were free-spirited rock 'n' roll musicians, and well...things sometimes got a little crazy out on the road.

With all their instruments and amps, the six or seven guys in the band—the number depended on the year—always travelled in at least two vehicles. Sometimes Rod was in the lead, sometimes it was Layne. The idea was to stay close enough to each other so that they'd arrive around the same time. If there was a mishap of any kind—flat tire, a hit deer, or running out of gas—the other car would be around to help out.

Most of the adventures told here come from a single, reliable source: Rod Norrie. Tales about travels with The Lincolns gush from their long-time drummer like water cascading over falls. On and on they come.

Let's begin with the night Rod lost sight of Layne's car behind him and began to check the rear-view mirror. At last, after a long delay, a pair of lights brightened the glass—it had to be Layne's car, coming up fast, intent on passing Rod.

"Look, he wants to play," Rod said to Frank MacKay, who was seated beside him.

Rod flattened the gas pedal, accelerating away, but Layne's car matched the move, taking after Rod. It was fun, Rod thought, until the car chasing him sounded its siren and showed flashing lights.

"That's not Layne," Rod cried out. No, indeed it was not.

Another time, Rod was coming back from Sackville well after midnight with Frank MacKay in the back seat and a third Lincoln up front, when they came upon the RCMP stopping cars

Rod Norrie loved playing drums for the band.
(DALHOUSIE UNIVERSITY ARCHIVES)

Don Muir played bass with the band for two full years, then switched to organ when John Gray moved on.
(COURTESY OF LAYNE FRANCIS)

at the intersection where drivers had to choose to go either to Prince Edward Island or to Nova Scotia. Rod slowed to a stop while Frank tidied up the beer bottles in the back seat.

"Whose beer is this?" the Mountie asked.

Frank claimed ownership because it would be better for him to take the rap for underage intoxication than for Rod to be charged with the much more serious offence of driving under the influence.

One police officer questioned Rod as he stood beside his car, while a second made Frank get out and bring the beer over to the police vehicle. Rod couldn't hear what was being said in that other conversation, but he was startled to see Frank begin to take the beer bottles out of the seized case and put them in the sleeves of his jacket. MacKay was taking The Lincolns's beer back! Rod made eye contact with Frank and shook his head vigorously. Frank understood and put the beer back into the case. Otherwise, in Rod Norrie's view, "the Mounties would have chased us to Truro."

Yet another time, The Lincolns were motoring in daylight along Highway 204 in the vicinity of West Leicester, Cumberland County. Layne and Rod knew that stretch of road well because of their many trips to play at Mount Allison University. They also knew there was rarely any traffic on that secondary high-way. As they entered what they knew to be a two-mile straight stretch with good visibility, Layne pulled out from behind Rod and came up alongside, their two vehicles filling both lanes. Young and foolish, each stepped on the gas. It was incredibly thrilling to be speeding side by side. Up ahead on the right, just off the road, was something neither driver could quite figure out. But whatever it was, it was remaining just off the road. At the speed they were going, the two cars came upon the mysterious shape very quickly. As they flashed by, they saw that it was a

The twin horns of Lee Taylor and Layne Francis gave The Lincolns a unique sound in the Maritimes in the 1960s; lead guitarist Frank Mumford, widely admired by other Maritime guitarists, more or less led the band in rehearsal.
(COURTESY OF LAYNE FRANCIS)

guy working a pit saw between two sawhorses right beside the highway. Layne and Rod flew by, like planes taking off. The scene was a blur, but each driver caught the look of utter shock on the poor guy's face as they swept past. "I can still see him," recalled Rod in 2018.

On another occasion, when a heavy snowfall was predicted, The Lincolns left Truro in the early afternoon to make sure they got to Sackville in time for their evening performance at Mount A. They thought they had left early enough, but the snow had other ideas. It came down fast and in abundance. By the time the two cars carrying the band were well into Cumberland County, they had to slow to a crawl, then come to a complete stop. And there they stayed. Their only hope was a Department of Highways plough.

It took a while—time the stalled musicians in their two cars spent sipping beer—but eventually a plough came along. The bad news was that it was doing the other side of the road, and behind came a parade of slow-moving cars and trucks. There was no way the band could slip over to that side and make tracks. They were stuck, unless—well, unless they could convince the driver of the plough to turn around and clear *their* side of the highway. It fell to Rod Norrie to make the pitch. He flagged down the driver and explained their predicament. The driver said he understood, but he had farther to go on his route before he would be coming back. It would be at least fifteen minutes.

"Hold on," said Rod. He hustled back to his car, retrieved a couple of quarts of beer, and returned to the plough, where he handed them to the driver.

"I'll see what I can do," the driver said. He was back in five minutes, clearing the road for The Lincolns.

It was ten o'clock before the band arrived in Sackville and got all set up and ready to play. The Mount A students were not too happy about the delay, but they had no idea how bad the roads were and how persuasive the musicians from Truro had to be to get there at all. Once the music began, the grumbling stopped.

And speaking of Mount A, one time a campus janitor spotted Lee Taylor giving himself an insulin injection for his diabetes. Jumping to the wrong conclusion, the janitor rushed to the university president, claiming that The Lincolns were shooting heroin. The matter was seen to right away, and quickly put to bed, when Lee explained what was in the needle.

Another of Rod's stories was of a hitchhiker the band picked up somewhere after leaving Sackville heading back to Truro. It was a freezing cold night, and Rod spotted the poor guy with his thumb out shivering by the side of the road. So, with space

IN THE WEE HOURS

Only when The Lincolns played in Halifax or Dartmouth did their getaway after a show or dance change. After they finished in a small town, they would quickly head back to Truro. But being close to the vibrant music scene in the Nova Scotia capital—especially the jazz and R & B clubs in city's North End—was an opportunity they seized. In the early years, it was the Arrows Club, later it might be the Gerrish Street Hall or the Club Unusual. It didn't matter that it was 12:30 or 1:00 when they arrived. The night was young and so were the musicians in The Lincolns. Recalling those North End hotspots, Frank MacKay said: "We would drop by to see Bucky Adams (tenor sax), Joe Sealy (piano), and usually Jack Harris (drums). These guys were the crème de la crème of the Halifax music after-hours scene. Joe was a keyboard player extraordinaire and did a lot of work with the CBC; Bucky was *the* jazz tenor cat, and Jack was the young up-and-comer, 'whiz kid' drummer."

Frank Mumford's favourite post-dance recollection was the night in 1967 that The Lincolns chanced to meet up with The Beach Boys. "They were playing in Halifax and we all ended up in an after-hours club, jamming till about five in the morning."

for one more in the car, Rod stopped to pick him up. It was the right thing to do, or so he thought. Making up for the stop, Rod recalled speeding up and going past a house on fire so fast the car probably fanned the flames. For the next hour The Lincolns partied on, with much beer drinking, laughter, stories, belches, and farts. It was how it was when The Lincolns travelled the road. Entertaining themselves in that customary manner, the band didn't notice that the hitchhiker was getting increasingly nervous. But they got the idea when he finally, and nervously, exclaimed: "This is good. This is good. Please let me out. It's only five miles to home. I can walk." Rod pulled over and let him out. And the band roared with laughter the moment the door closed and they sped away. Their good deed maybe wasn't quite so good after all.

Of the many noteworthy Lincoln road trip stories, the most famous one—thanks to John Gray's immortalizing it in his musical *Rock and Roll*—is where singer Frank MacKay got sick. The story, as Rod Norrie told it, begins with a gig at a formal dance at the Air Force Club in Moncton. The boys had made a special effort to dress for the occasion, renting two-piece suits from Truro's R. Trueman MacIntosh's Mens Wear: black-and-white houndstooth dress pants with black jackets and ties.

Following the dance, the trip home was eventful. "We were travelling past Sackville, New Brunswick, about two o'clock in the morning," recalled Rod in 2019. "I was driving my mother's brand new Chevrolet, with four or five people in the car, including Frank MacKay. Frank had been drinking all night and was not his usual self. He was feeling sick, very sick. And when he spoke up from the back seat to let me know how he felt, I warned him not to throw up in my mother's new car. I tried to slow down and pull over to the side of the road but Frank couldn't wait. He rolled down the window to throw up outside the car while it was whizzing along. Well, the wind in Frank's face did not comply.

What came shooting out didn't go far. Some froze to the side of the car; the rest came right back onto Frank. On his face and all over him, into the back seat and the back shelf."

Poor Frank had done his best. Poor Rod, his mother was not going to be pleased.

Two hours later, back in Truro, Rod dropped off his passengers, including Frank, at their homes before he began his search for someplace where he could clean the car. "It was the middle of the night, but I found Clary's twenty-four-hour taxi stand near the train station. It had a small garage, a dimly lit garage.

"Bill was the dispatcher for the taxi service and he was working the back shift. He was a nice, slow-moving man with a distinctive but endearing speech impediment. It was a slight stutter. He was in the process of sending one of the taxis to ' 'lev-'lev-'lev-eleven Revere Street' while puffing on a cigarette about a quarter-inch long, with two bits of tobacco hanging off the end. There was more smoke billowing out than I had ever seen."

Rod: "Bill, can you wash my car for me?"

Bill: "Yes. After I finish my game of ca-ca-ca-canasta."

Rod thought, it takes seven hours to play a game of canasta! "So I decided to wash the car myself. I had to get the car home before my mother had to leave for church.

"The garage had two bays, one with a grease pit with a car parked over it and the other I could use to wash my car. I drove my car into the empty bay and went back into the office to tell Bill that I was going to wash the car myself.

I walked back into the garage, around the front car that was parked over the grease pit, and the floor disappeared. I fell six feet down, thudding hard on the floor of the pit. Sweet mother of God! I hauled myself back up out of the pit, and in the light of the garage, I saw that I was covered from my shoes to my hair in mud, blood, grease, and beer."

In the late 1960s, lead singer Frank MacKay sported a shock of long hair, which seemed to fit the era and complement his soulful singing voice.

Bill heard the commotion and came out to see what had happened. His only comment: "Di-di-di-didn't you know it was there?"

Rod's rented suit was ruined, but he did get the car washed and home clean. Trueman MacIntosh had just made a sale of a pair of houndstooth pants and a black jacket. Never to be worn again.

Like the other band members, once the money started coming in pretty steadily, Frank MacKay decided to buy a car. The model he selected was a Mercury Cougar, which first went into production in 1967. Before Frank completed his first week as driver of the brand new car, he lost control on the North River Road, not far from where Rod Norrie lived. A horse ran onto the road, heading toward Frank's car. Frank swerved and hit a tree. Frank's insurance company judged the car a write-off but saw the singer placed in another Cougar right away. A week later, driving this replacement car on Elm Street in Truro after a Friday night Lincolns dance, Frank lost control once more. At approximately the same time, a kilometre or so away, fellow Lincoln Lee Taylor had an accident driving too fast in his bright yellow 1967 SS Chevelle on Smith Avenue.

In Frank MacKay's accident, his replacement Cougar tore the front porch off a house. With a pocket full of cash—about $100 in one dollar bills from his share of the night's dance receipts—Frank went up to the front door and handed it all over to pay for the damage he had done.

With two accidents in the space of a week, Frank decided he was through with cars. He did not drive another after that second accident. If there wasn't a friend to drive him where he was going, he used public transit.

Let's end our road recollections with the one that Frank MacKay said blew his mind. It was a trip in February 1969 to Saint John, where the Truro band was hired to play for a winter carnival event on the local campus of the University of New Brunswick. It was a new venue for the band, and all they knew about the slate of events was that Little Anthony and the Imperials, the renowned R & B and soul band out of New York City, were going to be playing the carnival as well. Everyone in the band knew Little Anthony's big hits, which included

"Hurt So Bad," "Tears on My Pillow," and "Goin' Out of My Head." The Lincolns were keen to see the celebrated American performer's show.

What The Lincolns encountered when they arrived in Saint John stunned Frank MacKay. Fifty years after the fact, he recalled: "It blew my mind. My favourite memory of The Lincolns.... We get up there on a Saturday and we're playing around 4:00 or 5:00 P.M. I'm figuring we're on first and then it'll be Little Anthony and the Imperials at 8:00 or 9:00 P.M. with their show. We're at the Barrack Green Armoury and the place is absolutely jammed. We didn't think anybody up there knew of us, but the place is jammed. I'd never seen anything like it. At least three thousand. We do our thing, including going down among the crowd with Layne on my shoulders."

The Lincolns's show ran its course, the huge audience of college and high school kids loving every minute. When it was over, Frank MacKay said to one of the winter carnival organizers: "I'd like to stick around now and see Little Anthony and the Imperials."

"Oh no," the guy replied, "they're not playing until tomorrow."

"Then it hit me," Frank remembered fifty years later. "All those kids were there to see us, The Lincolns. This was more than I had understood. We were why they were all there."

And then someone not with the band spread the word that The Lincolns were staying at the Admiral Beatty Hotel downtown and there was going to be a party. Hundreds of kids who had been at the show swarmed down the streets of Saint John to the hotel. The local police had to come and give the band an escort. They took The Lincolns around to the rear of the hotel to get them safely inside. Laughter in his voice, Frank MacKay said, "You would not believe it. You'd swear to God it was like

The Beatles. The people at the hotel were shaking their heads: 'How can we handle this?'"

In 1998, Frank Mumford also recalled that trip to Saint John as something special. He remembered the crowd at The Lincolns's show as being about four thousand. "It was quite the experience. It was a huge party. We spilled over into a downtown club and played all night. I still run into people who remember that night."

6

CHANGES,
CHANGES,
END

1968–69

*S*ooner or later, everyone realizes that the only constant in life is change. The ancient Greek philosopher Heraclitus (c. 535–475 BC) gets the credit for being the first to write that line, but countless others over the next 2,500 years discovered the same thing.

The 1960s were definitely about change, and the upheavals became more dramatic and transformative as the decade wore on. In 1968—the year I graduated from Truro Senior High and moved on to university—young people with long hair, hippie attire, and strong opinions seemed to be pretty much everywhere, at least in newspapers and magazines and on TV. Some of that zeitgeist made its way to Truro, altering clothing and hairstyles as well as the way some talked. "Say cool" and "Wha' say cool" replaced hi and hello as street greetings for a while. And we used "bread," "bummer," "dig it," "far out," "foxy," and "groovy" like we were jazz musicians. Inexplicably, many began talking about the signs of the zodiac, as if astrology could possibly make sense. Others turned to Tarot cards and the *I Ching*. I was among those who read Tolkein, Herman Hesse, Kurt Vonnegut, and

Richard Brautigan and watched National Film Board shorts and feature films by Ingmar Bergman. As Canadians, we were all pretty proud to claim Joni Mitchell, Leonard Cohen, and Gordon Lightfoot as our own. Practically everyone thought Bob Dylan was a demigod, and for a while he was just that. They were fun and zany times, and once the 1970s arrived, most of it disappeared like morning dew.

Young Canadians faced no draft and had little Canadian involvement in a foreign war to protest, but some wished they did. There was a certain cachet to emulating what young people in the United States and elsewhere in the world were seen doing on TV. And in 1968, that was head-spinning. All the turmoil certainly had its effect on me. When I arrived on the Dalhousie campus in September 1968, completely out of the blue I surprised myself by unexpectedly switching out of an intended Science major and ticking the block marked Arts. And so instead of a future in Math and Physics, I ended up in History—and trying to figure out the world around me by writing books. Maybe The Lincolns even had a hand in that, as I sought to find my own path to express myself.

Nineteen sixty-eight was also the year major changes hit Nova Scotia's favourite soul band—not the music they performed for dancing crowds, but the band's personnel. The changes were utterly unforeseen as the year began, and heartbreaking in different ways when they came to pass.

The story of the first change begins on a late February night in Halifax, and it starts off on a happy note. In fact, the night in question ranks at or near the top of all the memories Lincolns members have about their 1960s playing days.

We are in a ballroom at the Lord Nelson Hotel, a venue the band has never played before. It's as high-class and sophisticated as it gets in 1960s Halifax. Everyone is dressed in their very best clothes. The place is sold out, packed for a much anticipated Saint Mary's University event. It's started snowing outside, but inside the Lord Nelson it's warm and getting warmer. The speeches go on a bit too long, as they usually do, but at last—around ten o'clock—the band from Truro is ready to do its thing. The big ballroom fills with smiles from the opening notes. It only gets better after that. The Lincolns are rocking the place like it's the end of the world. In a good way.

One of those present is twenty-year-old Mary Clancy, who will go on to be a Halifax lawyer, a federal MP (1988–97), and Canada's consul general in Boston. It is now fifty years after that night in 1968, yet Mary still speaks fervently about it. "It's a memory with gold stars around it. An absolutely wonderful night, a magical night. Everybody had an amazing time. There was an electricity in the air. I would doubt there has ever been another night like it in Halifax. The music and the band were the absolute stars. They were the whole firmament."

Mary Clancy adds: "I do recall that I danced on a table. And not just one song. I commandeered the table for a while." Her date, she recalls, was more than a little nonplussed by her behaviour. Oh well, rocking to R & B really wasn't his thing. He later decided to become a priest.

In case you're wondering, yes, the band does notice the young woman, Mary Clancy, dancing on the table. But they have hundreds of other attendees to take in as well, and as far as The Lincolns can see, everyone in the ballroom is having a blast. So the band does what it always did: it keeps the music coming. That includes the bit where Frank MacKay puts sax-playing Layne Francis on his shoulders and does a tour of the room. The crowd loves it. They love everything The Lincolns do that night at the Lord Nelson.

Mary Clancy had heard The Lincolns play before that Saint Mary's event, but "this was the first time I heard the full power of them. The sound was unique. They were an absolutely wonderful band. It was one of those dances where everybody danced all the time. Their music just flowed through you. And there was this incredible sense of fun and joy. Being young and dancing with abandon and listening to this marvellous music by these incredibly charismatic band members, that was when you really understood the magic of rock music."

As if that is not praise enough, Mary Clancy says this: "The Lincolns were the best band I ever heard in Halifax and one of the best bands, period. They had an incredible chemistry. They took American rock 'n' roll and made it their own. It made them unique. They had something nobody else had. A totally one-of-a-kind band." She firmly believes that the Truro-based band, through its many region-wide performances, helped "open the door to what has become the Nova Scotia music scene."

There is one more comment from my telephone interview with Mary Clancy that I want to include: "I went to Europe a few months later, and I feel that I was more adventuresome on that trip because of that night. The Lincolns helped me find a new part of my personality."

Reading that reflection again—and having heard Mary Clancy say it with conviction in our telephone interview—I wonder how many others feel the same way she does. I don't just mean about that night at the Lord Nelson, but in all the other communities The Lincolns played in over their span of years. How many others felt that listening/dancing/watching/responding to that particular band changed some part of their personality? After all, The Lincolns put everything they had into their shows. They were all in, each and every time, and audiences everywhere loved them for it. My guess is that twenty-year-old Mary Clancy was not alone in feeling transformed. My hunch is that hundreds, if not thousands, of young people had their own personal connecting moments with The Lincolns. Which is why, for decades after, so many people were so utterly keen to talk about the band and snap up tickets for reunions.

Well, all good things must end, including that electricity-charged Saint Mary's event at the Lord Nelson. It is past one o'clock on Sunday morning when the last note fades away. As the crowd reluctantly files out, The Lincolns start to pack up their stuff, a process that takes a good hour thanks to all the gear—and especially the two-hundred-kilogram Hammond. Once everything is safely stowed in the truck, the band starts out for Truro, except for Frank Mumford, who lives in Halifax. Don Muir and Lee Taylor are in the truck, while Rod Norrie is driving everyone else in his car, a 1965 Ford station wagon, leading the way.

The snow that had been coming down lightly when The Lincolns walked into the Lord Nelson hours earlier has not stopped. By the time the band gets on the road, around two o'clock, between fifteen and eighteen centimetres is down. It's going to be a long, slow drive home.

Rod Norrie checks his rear-view mirror occasionally, making sure the truck with the gear is not far behind. Sure enough, the truck's headlights are always there—all along old Highway 2 through Enfield, Shubenacadie, Stewiacke, and beyond. Then suddenly, just past the crossroads for Alton, close to Shortts Lake, the headlights disappear. Rod slows to a stop at the bottom of the hill on the snow-covered slippery road. Carefully, he negotiates a tricky turnaround, then guides the station wagon back up the hill to find out where the pickup truck has gone.

At the top of the hill, Rod and his passengers find Don Muir and Lee Taylor standing in the middle of the road. They look to be all right, but the truck they were driving is out in an adjacent field!

Don Muir describes what happened: "I was driving the pick-up, Roddie's truck, and Lee and I were chatting on the way home. I got into a tire rut from a truck and it pulled me off the road. We weren't going fast—it just gradually pulled us. I couldn't get stopped and I couldn't steer. We just slowly went into the ditch."

The truck had stayed on its wheels, but it went down into the ditch and then up and out into a field, with Don and Lee escaping without a scratch. Rod, whose truck it was, was relieved that his friends were unhurt and drove to a nearby garage. It was closed, but there was a payphone. He called Goodspeeds towing service in Truro. Then he and his fellow Lincolns went home. Sometime later, the tow truck arrived and brought the vehicle into Truro.

The mishap was minor, barely worth remembering, except for what happened next. A few hours later, around eight o'clock that Sunday morning (February 25, 1968), Lee Taylor went into a diabetic coma. He was taken to the hospital in Truro and hooked up to machines to keep him alive. Since he was not injured in the accident, it must have been that, in the excitement of the past twenty-four hours, he had missed one or more shots of insulin.

While Lee's condition was a cause for worry, the expectation within the band and the wider Truro community was that the diminutive sax player would come around in a day or two. The Lincolns, individually and as a group, went often to visit him. Don Muir recalled some of the banter: "'C'mon, wake up, Lee. What about Friday night?' We were hoping he was in there somewhere, listening."

Lee Taylor's condition did not change as the week went on. Then it worsened, and he was transferred to the Victoria General Hospital in Halifax.

Lee Taylor, shown here between Layne Francis and Frank MacKay, was a beloved member of The Lincolns; his sudden passing shook the band.
(COURTESY OF LAYNE FRANCIS)

On Friday, March 1, 1968, the Lincolns dance went ahead as usual at the Truro Legion—well, not quite as usual, because there was only Layne Francis on sax. Then, around the time of the evening when the band usually took its first break, the Truro police received a phone call. Policeman Frank Burke got the job to tell The Lincolns first, and then to go to the microphone on-stage to inform the crowd: Lee Taylor had died.

Maxine Wallace, who was in the crowd that night, recalled the "terrible sadness" down on the floor. Like The Lincolns, the fans were in shock. The dance was cancelled immediately. Singer Frank MacKay was struck by how "the crowd left the building out of respect."

Layne Francis, who had played sax alongside Lee for years, said he "cried that night—it was a terrible blow to all of us. It was never the same again, having that little guy play that big sax."

Victor Lee Taylor was only twenty-two when he passed away, but he packed an enormous amount of living into that short span. His brief obituary identified him as a son of Mr. and Mrs. Percy Taylor of Harmony Road, and as an employee of the Waverley Construction Company who was also "a member of a local band." Whoever wrote that clearly had no idea how important The Lincolns truly had been in Lee's life.

Layne's comment that "it was never the same again" after Lee died is an understatement. The rest of 1968 would see many more changes in the makeup of The Lincolns. It was to be a year of multiple transitions.

The band moved quickly to find a second saxophone. Layne selected Richard "Dick" Snook, who had come up through the Truro school band program directed by Ron MacKay. Dick had begun playing clarinet as a kid, then moved over to the saxophone. When the call came from The Lincolns, it was a huge surprise. Dick recalled in late 2018: "One day I'm playing in our garage band with Phisch [Gregg Fancy], Camshaft [Keith MacInnis], Greg Bell, and a couple of others; the next weekend I'm at the Legion with The Lincolns." It was a big leap. Dick was still in high school at the time and living at home. The extra income, plus the excitement of playing before the band's thousand or so adoring fans felt pretty good. (Phisch Fancy, by the way, would later play with The Lincolns himself and go on to an extremely successful musical career with the Dutch Mason Blues Band and other groups. Keith MacInnis would also play professionally, most recently with Over the Influence.)

Not long after Dick Snook joined the band, he and the rest of The Lincolns were on CBC TV. The show was called *Where It's At*, hosted by one-time Truro deejay Frank Cameron. Another guest on the program was soon-to-be international singing star Anne Murray. Footage of the entire hour-long program broadcast

Dick Snook, Layne Francis, and John MacLachlan Gray at the 1978 reunion.
(COURTESY OF ELEANOR AND ROD NORRIE)

on April 9, 1968, still exists in the CBC archives. Previously, The Lincolns had been ·on two other Halifax-produced shows, *Frank's Bandstand* and *Let's Go*, but none of those broadcasts appears to have survived.

As directed by CBC, The Lincolns put on special attire—clothes they never wore at any of their dances. All but Frank MacKay wore long-sleeved turtlenecks, all different bright colours, with sneakers on their feet. Frank wore a loose dress shirt and a scarf. Everyone wore makeup and had their hair attended to.

As was typical on all such shows at the time, the songs were pre-recorded, with the performers pretending to play and sing during the actual filming. By themselves, The Lincolns performed "Nobody Knows," "Cry to Me," and "You've Got Me Hummin'." In addition, Frank MacKay, backed by the show's

The Imperials, 1964: (left to right) Barry Ryan (bass), Bill Crowe (guitar), Glenn Irving (drums), Jack Miller (vocals), and Greg Langille (guitar).
(PRIDHAM'S STUDIO)

house band, sang "If I Were a Carpenter" and "Shoo Be Doo Be Doo Da Day" with Doug Billard. As well, The Lincolns were the backup band as Anne Murray sang Aretha Franklin's "Baby, I Love You." Everyone involved in the show took part in the finale, "I Dig Rock 'n' Roll."

The Lincolns would appear on more TV shows in the months ahead.

Incidentally, the drummer in the house band for "Where It's At"—a band called The New Five Sounds plus One—was Jack Lilly, who also played drums on the *Frank's Bandstand* and *Singalong Jubilee* TV shows, and who would soon enter the story of The Lincolns as well.

The composition of The Lincolns changed again when organist John Gray left to pursue an MA in Theatre at the University of British Columbia. From there, he would go on to have a remarkable career in theatre and fiction—more about that later. With John's leaving, bass player Don Muir moved over to play the Hammond. Don had been practising on the organ for months on his own time, coming to the Legion after school every chance he got. Self-taught, Don became better than adequate; he mastered the keyboard, and The Lincolns didn't miss a beat.

Moving onto bass guitar with Don's shift to organ was Barry Ryan. Barry had turned down that option back in 1965 but not in the spring of 1968. The Lincolns were soaring in popularity across the region, and he jumped at the chance to be part of it. He had idolized Frank Mumford since he was a young teen. Back then, watching The Lincolns play at the Pleasant Street Hall, Barry's friends (including Don Muir) used to call Barry "little Frank." That was because he dressed like, did his hair like, and rolled up his sleeves like his hero. As Barry recollected in 2019: "I would sit beside the stage and watch Frank Mumford play guitar, and memorize as much as I could, then I would go home right after the dance and pick up my guitar and practise what I had seen him play. I did this every Friday night." Finally, in 1968, Barry started playing alongside the musician he most admired. Thinking back to his move into the band, Barry Ryan recalled how much he still learned from Frank Mumford. When Barry occasionally lost his focus on some song, Mumford brought him back with a glare that said, "Pay attention." Barry has never forgotten that lesson.

It's a lesson that merits further comment, because it sums up The Lincolns onstage. It was not in their nature ever just to mail it in. They were all in for every performance, no matter where they played. Although their repertoire was mostly R & B and soul songs they had not written themselves, the guys in the band respected and loved that material—and performed their own versions to the maximum of their abilities. To be in the band, you not only had to have talent; you also had to "pay attention," as Frank Mumford put it, or "sing it and play it like you mean it," as Frank MacKay had said to his bandmates in Ontario. Their musicianship, combined with the intensity and joy of their performances, made a Lincolns dance an experience never to be forgotten. They were an art form all their own, one in which the fans down on the floor played a vital supporting role.

The Lincolns had become undeniable stars on the Maritime music scene. They were constantly in demand, and the pay they requested was steadily climbing. Toronto artist Ian Murray recalled that, back in his student days at the Nova Scotia College of Art and Design (NSCAD) in Halifax, he was on a committee trying to book The Lincolns. "It was $3,200 for the Truro band and $3,000 for Sam and Dave backed by Booker T and the MGs." Adjusting for inflation, that $3,200 figure converts to just over $21,000 today!

Whether it was the band's mounting success—which might have sparked ideas of taking The Lincolns beyond the Maritimes—or Lee Taylor's passing, or simply the surrounding spirit of change of the time, another dramatic transition was fast approaching for the Truro-based band.

Unknown to Rod Norrie, the drummer who had been with the band from its inception, lead guitarist Frank Mumford had come to the conclusion that The Lincolns now needed someone other than Rod on drums. Rock 'n' roll was changing, becoming more jazz-influenced and sophisticated, with groups like Chicago and Blood, Sweat & Tears. That was the direction Mumford saw The Lincolns moving in, and at least some of the other members of the group agreed. The problem from Mumford's perspective was that he didn't think Rod had the technical proficiency on drums for the more complicated songs. Rod had been with the group through thick and thin for years and was the big-hearted friend to all of them. But now Mumford wanted to move Rod aside—specifically, he wanted Jack Lilly, the versatile drummer who was on three different CBC TV shows.

Rod Norrie knew nothing about any of this, but he had picked up that something had soured in his friendship with Frank Mumford. The two of them had long been as close as brothers—as had everyone in the band. How could they not? They all had spent more time together and shared more experiences than with anyone else. But as the year unfolded, Rod could tell that Frank Mumford was ticked off with him. He thought it was because he had spoken up when the lead guitarist asked for his travel to and from Truro to be reimbursed and Rod objected. Rod felt—and said as much—that he and Layne Francis had used their own vehicles for years to drive the band with only a small reimbursement ever coming from the rest of the band. Rod could see that his objections did not sit well with the guitarist, who also functioned as the band's conductor, but he had no inkling of what was about to happen.

Looking back on 1968 from the perspective of 2019, Rod recalled that, "following one of the weekly rehearsals at the Legion, Frank asked me to step outside. He wanted to talk." The minute they were alone, Frank told Rod that they were replacing him as The Lincolns's drummer with Jack Lilly. "I admit Jack is the better drummer," said Rod, "but I was deeply hurt, angry, and disappointed. Frank Mumford was a close friend and, like me, one of the original Lincolns. I am certain that it was mainly because of the money issue."

I asked both Frank MacKay and Don Muir about the switch of drummer, but neither wanted to say much about it, other than to talk generally about how rock 'n' roll was changing and that Jack Lilly had more expertise. When I spoke to Jack Lilly about his entry into The Lincolns, he told me he had met with

Jack Lilly playing at the 1978 Lincolns reunion.
(COURTESY OF ELEANOR AND ROD NORRIE)

the band before Frank Mumford broke the news to Rod. Jack also said that Mumford told him that "replacing Roddie was the hardest decision I ever made."

Incredibly, at the end of that short conversation between Mumford and Rod outside the Legion, Frank told Rod "that if I wanted to play at the Truro Golf Club dance the coming weekend, it could be my last night I would play with the band." Rod replied in no uncertain terms that—well, you can fill in the blanks. He could not get over that his old friend had waited until after he had gone through a full practice before telling him he was being replaced.

One might think that episode would have permanently poisoned Rod's friendship with Frank Mumford, and maybe with the rest of the band. Yet it did not. Rod was able to move on.

Despite being dropped, he continued to regard Frank as a close friend, and their two families continued to spend time together. And when the parade for the Nova Scotia Provincial Exhibition was held in Truro in late August 1968, who do you think drove the truck that pulled the float carrying The Lincolns and Anne Murray? It was Rod Norrie! Incidentally, The Lincolns were all dressed as hillbillies on that float, some of them as women.

As for Anne Murray, she was barefoot all week—her look at the time. "Barefoot and beautiful" was how she was introduced every time to the Exhibition stage. Two years before "Snowbird" would make her an international star, she was already well-known across the Maritimes from her many TV appearances on *Singalong Jubilee*, *Let's Go*, and other shows. During that exhibition week in Truro, Anne Murray, backed by The Lincolns, performed daily. Anne had arrived in Truro a couple of days before to rehearse with the band at the Colchester Stadium. Frank MacKay and Anne even sang a few duets. When I contacted Anne in 2019 to see if she recalled the songs she sang that week, she replied that "A Little Bit of Soap" was definitely one, and maybe "Unchained Melody." Beyond that, "it's just so long ago—and a lot of songs ago." She added, "The Lincolns were a great band. We had a fantastic week together at the provincial exhibition."

Though Rod Norrie was no longer a Lincoln, he went out of his way to make sure that Anne Murray felt suitably welcomed by Truro. He hosted a barbecue at the Norrie family farm to which the singer from Springhill *and* The Lincolns and their partners were all invited. In addition, Rod convinced the exhibition organizers to have Anne present a trophy in the horse ring. Rod accompanied her to the event.

In the early months of 1969, the band's renown continued to spread far and wide, especially on college campuses. Cited earlier as an example was the show they gave in Saint John,

New Brunswick, in February, where they thrilled three to four thousand fans and touched off a mini-riot at their hotel. A couple of months later, in Halifax, there was another epic night at the Dalhousie University Student Union Building. The band used to play there a lot, sometimes on a Wednesday, sometimes on a Saturday.

On this particular spring night, it was the 1969 Graduation Dance. For Barry Ryan, it stood out as "one of the best nights that I ever played with The Lincolns.... The main hall was totally packed with about six to eight hundred people, so they set up a camera on the band and put a screen on the stage downstairs, in the hall directly below us, and put another six hundred-plus people in that hall, and piped the music in over a PA system in that room, plus the video image of us playing upstairs." The arrangement was working fine, but then Frank MacKay and Layne Francis decided to mix in some special fun, bringing out an old familiar trick with a brand new twist. In Barry Ryan's words: "We were playing 'Mustang Sally,' and about halfway through the song Frank put Layne on his shoulders and went around the room, with Layne playing sax, while we continued to play. Then Frank and Layne got on the elevator, which was in the room where we were playing. It took them to the room downstairs, to the other six hundred people. Out of the elevator came Layne on Frank's shoulders, still playing sax, while the sound of the band playing upstairs was coming through the PA system. They paraded around the downstairs floor for seven or eight minutes, and then the elevator doors opened again in the hall upstairs where we were still playing 'Mustang Sally.' Back up onstage they came, and Layne got off of Frank's shoulders at that time. We ended up playing 'Mustang Sally' for almost twenty minutes that night, and the crowd—two separate crowds—went wild! It was an amazing night!"

It was classic Lincolns: taking a familiar song and making it into their own for the maximum enjoyment of their paying customers. The episode underlines how and why The Lincolns had become the Maritimes' top 1960s band. They delivered great music as well as an unmatched entertainment presence. For many months during this period, the Truro-based band added to its distinctive sound by having, in addition to the usual twin saxes, John Gray's younger brother Charlie play trumpet.

In the spring or early summer of 1969, the band suddenly underwent another major change. Out of the blue, Frank Mumford told his bandmates that he'd had enough. He was married, with two daughters, and he had a full-time job in Halifax as a claims examiner. The constant travel for the band was a strain. Recalled Frank: "I was getting worn down, working all day and then all night. Plus, I had a family I wasn't spending enough time with." What Frank Mumford told Don Muir was this: "I don't want to do it anymore. I want to be a family man."

With Mumford's departure, Barry Ryan moved over to play lead guitar, a role he used to have with The Imperials. Into the band to take over from Barry on bass came Gregg "Phisch" Fancy, who had also been with The Imperials. Like Barry (and Don Muir before him), Phisch had grown up watching The Lincolns and had hurried home after dances to practise pieces he had watched them play. "The Lincolns were my idols," he recalled in 2019. "I felt blessed to finally play with them."

Maybe The Lincolns in this latest constellation would have lasted another year or more, but we'll never know. Not long after Frank Mumford left, two strangers showed up one Friday night at the Truro Legion, and soon The Lincolns were winding down. I remember seeing the two of them standing in the centre of the dance floor. I didn't know who they were at first, but it was obvious they were not local—by how they dressed and how they

Three of Truro's Imperials in 1965: lead guitarist Barry Ryan holding his 1954 Fender Strat, drummer Glenn Irving holding his sticks, and, seated on the floor, bass guitarist Gregg "Phisch" Fancy. Barry would join The Lincolns in 1968 and Phisch for a month or so in 1969. All three would play many times with the band at various Lincolns reunions.
(CHARLIE AWAD)

held themselves in the centre of the Legion floor. They seemed to be studying The Lincolns as though there was an audition underway—which, it turned out, there was, sort of.

Sometime later I found out that the two strangers were Bob Murphy and Donnie Morris. They had both started out in the early 1960s in different Nova Scotia bands before joining with others in 1966 to form the Toronto-based Stitch In Tyme. That group had had some notable success, such as playing at Expo '67 and having a nationwide hit with their cover of The Beatles's "Got to Get You Into My Life." By 1969, however, The Stitch In Tyme was no more. Murphy and Morris were back in their home province looking to be involved in something else. And that something else involved The Lincolns. Or, rather, about half the band.

On more than one occasion during that summer of 1969, Morris and Murphy went backstage at the Legion during intermission to speak to The Lincolns. Those conversations quickly got to the point: Murphy and Morris wanted three of The Lincolns to join what they were seeing as a brand new band. As Don Muir explained, "They started talking to Frank, Layne, and I, and they convinced us that we should start a new band and go to Toronto. It had never occurred to me to do that until these two guys came along."

The idea was that the new band would move away from the soul and R & B repertoire that The Lincolns played and toward a more jazz-influenced, heavy guitar sound. It was thought they would attract other top musicians—such as guitarist Ritchie Oakley and drummer Jack Harris—to create a supergroup that would write original material. The name of that new band was not picked right away, but it eventually would be Soma, the name of the drug in Aldous Huxley's dystopian novel, *Brave New World*. Why someone would pick such a name puzzled me at the time, as it does now. Had Bob Murphy ever read the book? Soma, in that futuristic literary world, has a mind-numbing effect.

In retrospect, it's not hard to understand how and why Frank MacKay, Layne Francis, and Don Muir were won over by the idea of playing with Soma. The prospect of finding a new style and writing their own material, not to mention performing before even bigger crowds beyond the Maritimes, must have been attractive. Just as important, the band they had known and loved for years—The Lincolns and The New Lincolns—was no longer what it once was. Lee Taylor had died, Rod Norrie had been dismissed,

John Gray had left, and Frank Mumford had quit. Frank, Layne, and Don were the only members who went back to before 1968. So, without much hesitation, the singer, saxophonist, and organist decided to take the leap. When they announced their decision to their bandmates, Jack Lilly was the only one to speak up. Don Muir remembered Jack saying: "Ah, guys, you don't have to do this. Why be a small fish in a big city when you can be a big fish in a small city here in Nova Scotia?"

Jack's question did not alter their decision. Don, Layne, and Frank continued to play with The Lincolns through that summer, but the word was out: they were simultaneously practising and developing new material with Soma. Soma's bass player, Donnie Morris, took over from Phisch Fancy on that instrument for The Lincolns for the rest of the summer.

As I recall, Lincolns fans were sorry to learn that the dances at the Legion were coming to an end, yet excited to think that three Lincolns were joining a hot new band that was going to conquer the world. Like hockey fans who, decades later, cheered when Sydney Crosby and Nathan MacKinnon made it to the NHL, the band's devotees liked the idea of Frank, Layne, and Donnie playing in music's bigger leagues.

And so The Lincolns slowly wound down, with their final performance in September 1969. Meanwhile, out in Portapique (at an old house owned by Bob Murphy's mother), Soma took shape. Don Muir recalled a trip out there on one of the last Friday nights he played with The Lincolns at the Legion. In keeping with a number of other tales in this book, this one, too, involves cars and booze. It begins with Don driving down to an Island bootlegger before heading out to Portapique. Coming past the Goodspeeds car dealership with a bottle of wine, he was stopped by Truro policeman Albert Jackson. Jackson took the wine and gave Don a ticket for $13.50: Truro was still a "dry"

Layne Francis and Don Muir singing harmony.
(DALHOUSIE UNIVERSITY ARCHIVES)

town at that point. Don waited ten minutes until he thought the coast should be clear, then returned to the Island. In hiding and waiting for him was Albert Jackson. "I watched you go down there," the policeman explained as he held out his hand for Don to give him the second bottle of wine. Don decided not to try a third time but headed out empty-handed to join his Soma friends.

As for that new band, I'll leave the story of Soma to someone else. Suffice it to say that Soma's beginning was The Lincolns's end. Soma premiered its initial material in early October 1969 in a barn outside Truro. The place was packed with former Lincolns fans, all curious to see and hear what the new band would be like. I was there among the throng for one of the two shows. I have to say that Soma's musicians—thirteen of them at that point; they would later slim down to five—were good. Very good—likely the best in Atlantic Canada at the time. Everyone in my circle wished them well. But quietly, among ourselves, the old equation surrounding The Lincolns still held: We were theirs = They were ours.

There was nothing Soma or any other band could do to change that. After all, many of us had danced to The Lincolns a hundred times. We'd seen Soma and heard their new songs once or twice.

In the normal story of a rock 'n' roll band, that would be the end of the tale. The Lincolns, however, were no ordinary band. It turned out that they were far from done. Not for another fifty years.

In my late twenties, I was living in Sydney, Nova Scotia, and working as a historian at the Fortress of Louisbourg, when I heard news I could scarcely believe. Friends in Truro were saying there was talk that, after nearly a decade apart, The Lincolns were coming back together. For two nights. It was said to be Rod Norrie's idea: a fundraiser for minor football, with the dances to be held at the Teachers' College. Right away I called Jack Manning at his music store on Truro's Inglis Street to set aside two tickets. It was going to be good.

Or was it? The band hadn't been a band for a long time. Each musician had gone his own separate way following the dissolution. Yes, some were still active on the music scene, playing all the time, but others hadn't touched their instruments in years. Didn't groups have to play together frequently to sound good? Maybe a reunion was a bad idea, something that could tarnish people's cherished memories of how good the powerhouse band had once been.

The Lincolns take a break from rehearsals for the 1978 reunion: (left to right, front row) Frank MacKay, Jack Lilly, Don Muir, equipment technician Barry "Scrapper" Stevenson, and Brian Chisholm; (back row) Barry Ryan, John MacLachlan Gray, Frank Mumford, Dick Snook, Layne Francis, equipment technician Vernon Daley, and Rod Norrie.

Some of The Lincolns, it turns out, were having the same qualms as the reunion approached. Here is what organist-turned-playwright John MacLachlan Gray writes in *Local Boy Makes Good*: "We sensed that we could be making fools of ourselves, which was a grim prospect, for the band was an important memory to all of us. There was something about that time that we knew we would never know again, that we didn't want to see desecrated." John goes on to recall what it had been like for him to be a Lincoln from 1966 to 1968. "For me The Lincolns represent one of life's miracles. A group of unexceptional teenaged

Layne Francis (in the background) and drummer Rod Norrie during the 1978 reunion—two of the original Lincolns.
(COURTESY OF ELEANOR AND ROD NORRIE)

males, from different classes, religions, and parts of town... attracting audiences of up to a thousand with no agent and no recording contract. The Lincolns were stars."

And so they were again—stars, that is—for two warm and glorious nights in early September 1978. All the old Lincolns showed up, including those who had once been dropped from the band. Any past hard feelings melted away. Each acquitted himself well, from drums to keyboards, and from the horns to the man belting out the lyrics: the incomparable Frank MacKay. To everyone's joy, and relief, the band was, in John Gray's words, "still the best band around." That was because "The Lincolns was *their band*. We finished the concert with what can only be described as a feeling of lightness, a sense that a perceived weight was the common property of a great many people." And further, John had a eureka moment: "I knew there was a musical there somewhere."

If anyone in the Canada of 1978 could recognize the germ of a musical, it was John MacLachlan Gray. His first major musical, *Eighteen Wheels*, was already touring the country, and *Billy Bishop Goes to War* was about to do the same, even more successfully while winning a slew of honours. Inspired by his 1960s experiences with The Lincolns, as magnified and distilled by the 1978 reunion, John was soon to write *Rock and Roll*, starring none other than Frank MacKay in the lead role. As John says in the foreword to this book: "I had no Plan B—it just had to be him."

The musical opened at the National Arts Centre in Ottawa in 1981 and presented the story of a band called The Monarchs, the stars of a small town called Mushaboom. As in any artistic creation, the characters in the play are not exactly Gray's old actual bandmates in The Lincolns, but composites, and enhanced. Nonetheless, to anyone who grew up in Truro, *Rock and Roll* is about their town and their favourite band, The Lincolns. At the same time, Gray turns a local story into something universal that people anywhere could relate to and love. The musical was a hit and toured Canada in 1983. In 1985, an adaptation became an award-winning TV movie on CBC with the title *The King of Friday Night*. In the process, The Lincolns moved from being admired and celebrated in the 1960s to attaining legendary status in the 1980s.

For Frank MacKay, the lead in *Rock and Roll* would be just the start of a busy and much praised acting career. Over the next twenty years, he would star in a couple of dozen plays and musicals, including as Jean Valjean in the Neptune Theatre, Halifax, production of *Les Misérables*. He would also write a few screenplays and at least one play, *The Red Row*, which told the story of his early years in Stellarton. And when not acting onstage, Frank continued to sing around the Maritimes and for a while in Calgary. From time to time, there were also reunions with his beloved Lincolns.

Those reunions followed no particular pattern: they happened when they happened, most often for a fundraiser in Truro. At each, Frank MacKay and all the other musicians enlisted became Lincolns for a night or two. They always gave kick-ass performances, which kept fans clamouring for more. Most of the surviving old bandmates—Francis, Lilly, MacKay, Muir, Mumford, Norrie, and Ryan—would be there, joined sometimes by players such as Phisch Fancy, Jeff Goodspeed, Dawn Hatfield, Glenn Irving, and Shirley Jackson. Whichever combination it was on any given night, The Lincolns rocked whatever venue they played. The songs were always the same old 1960s soul and R & B tunes, and they performed them more or less as they always had, lengthening them with solos or when Frank MacKay chose to get the entire crowd to sing along on certain songs (like "Mustang Sally"). You might think the reunions were just for fun, and therefore relaxed affairs, but the musicians always performed as though their lives (and musical reputations) depended on how much professionalism and intensity they delivered. That's how it had always been with The Lincolns, and that's how it remained.

Importantly, The Lincolns continued to be an influence. Here is what Charlie A'Court, a multiple ECMA and Music Nova Scotia award winner, recalled when contacted in early 2019: "In the summer of '94 I was fifteen and not allowed into a 'reunion' show Frank MacKay and The Lincolns were putting on at the Legion. My dad and I sat outside on the bank next to the back emergency door listening to the band laying it down inside. We couldn't see anything, but man alive—we sang along to every song like we were in the front row. When I heard Frank bellow out "I've Got Dreams to Remember" for the first time, that's when I knew what I wanted to be when I grew up."

I was out of the country for the reunion in 2017, but I made sure I got my tickets early—nine months ahead—when another

Part of the crowd at 1978 reunion show.
(COURTESY OF ELEANOR AND ROD NORRIE)

was announced for September 2018. This time round, the band was going to be back at the Legion for the first time in nearly fifty years for what the tickets said was "One Last Time."

Just as John MacLachlan Gray confesses in the foreword, I too worried that this was going to be one performance too many. Sooner or later, everything has a best-before date. By 2018, all the original Lincolns were close to or in their seventies. Could they really keep turning the clock back as they had always done?

Miraculously, that's exactly what the band did, on two successive nights. With minimal preparation, but drawing on their deep-seated musicianship and some mysterious force of life, the 2018 Lincolns gave two terrific performances. The band was bigger than it had ever been, with four horns, two keyboards, a rotation of three drummers, lead guitar, and bass. And of course, the one and only Frank MacKay up front directing the whole show. It was hard to believe. Dream-like. A dream to remember, in fact. It was as if we had all been transported back to 1968.

When the shows were over, everyone wondered when, not if, another Lincolns performance would be organized. After all,

The September 2018 performances by The Lincolns, back at the Truro Legion for the first time since 1969, thrilled the crowds.
(A. J. B. JOHNSTON)

the guys up onstage were apparently immortal. Could they do it again the following year? When I posed that question separately to Rod Norrie and Frank MacKay in late 2018, both smiled. "You never know," each said.

Sadly, Frank MacKay died on March 6, 2019, after open-heart surgery. It is now inconceivable that The Lincolns will ever perform again. Not without that dynamic, driving personality and golden voice out front. Of the original five, only Rod and Layne remain. So the story of The Lincolns's live performances has almost certainly come to an end, sixty years after it began.

Or so I thought, before attending the Celebration of Life for Frank MacKay in May 2019. That afternoon at Halifax's Marquee Club, listening to guest singers Sam Moon, Wayne Nicholson, and Charlie A'Court fill in for Frank, backed by the latest cast of The Lincolns, I realized that a new version of the band could indeed still materialize on special occasions—like a rock 'n' roll phoenix. It might even be fitting for the legendary band, considering how resilient and adaptable the original Lincolns were. The music should go on.

Predicting the future, however, is not my thing. I'd rather try to sum up what made The Lincolns of the 1960s so appealing that they are passionately remembered a half-century later. As I see it, it comes down to this: across the span of that decade, up and down Nova Scotia and into New Brunswick, the Truro-based band helped establish a viable and exciting Maritime music scene. They did it the only way they knew how, by developing their own art form. That art was to play a trademark brand of music with intensity and joy, connecting with thousands of fans at live music shows. Humming with a collective life force and a distinct sound, which showcased twin saxes, an organ, and Frank MacKay, The Lincolns filled and thrilled countless halls. In the Maritimes of the 1960s, there

Bruce MacKinnon's editorial cartoon in the Halifax Chronicle Herald, *March 9, 2019.*

(COURTESY OF THE CHRONICLE HERALD AND BRUCE MACKINNON)

was no other band anything like them. And because of the music they "played—"Join in the Soul" was their brand—they attracted diverse crowds. In that way, The Lincolns ignored and dismissed racial barriers and brought communities together that until then had mostly been apart.

One more thing: because The Lincolns played frequently at certain venues—Truro's Legion, Dartmouth High, Mount Allison University, and the Dalhousie Student Union Building—a bond developed between the guys up onstage and the dancers down below. Hundreds, if not thousands, of loyal fans knew The Lincolns's songlist as well as the musicians themselves. Long-term memory lays down deep tracks, which is why so many 1960s diehards are still so keen to groove in front of the band as they used to do. It's a sweet and soulful form of time travel.

In early 2019, in my final interviews with the main Lincolns of the 1960s, I asked each how he would sum up his feelings for the old band in a single word. Layne Francis, jazz player that he is, chose not to colour within my suggested lines. Instead of a single word, he responded with three short phrases: "Those were the days," "Best years of my life," and "What a band!"

The others did play along with me, keeping it to a single word.

Rod Norrie's instant reply was "Lucky," referring to the many wonderful times he and his bandmates had enjoyed.

For Don Muir, the word that came immediately over the phone was "Love." Being a Lincoln, he explained, "was the first time I was ever accepted for being me."

As for Frank MacKay, speaking to me a month before he died, he chose "Appreciation." He explains why in the afterword.

Long live The Lincolns! And live music everywhere!

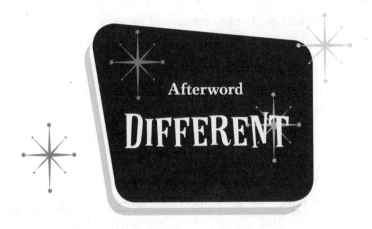

Afterword

DIFFERENT

What do they mean by different? And how could they know?
These feelings I keep to myself; I've never let them show...
- FROM THE SONG "DIFFERENT" BY FRANK MACKAY

Author's Note: *Over a span of six months, I sat down twice with Frank MacKay for long interviews. We also exchanged many emails about different aspects of his life and times with The Lincolns. In January 2019, I asked him if he would consider writing an afterword. Frank said he would. When, a few weeks later, I inquired how it was going, he sent me the first half of what is below. Less than a week later, Frank was suddenly gone, dying from heart failure. Cleaning up Frank's apartment after his passing, Dawn Hatfield, his niece and a saxophonist at numerous Lincolns reunions, found the longer version published below.*

As you will see, Frank's piece is not quite finished, but he was getting close. He had arrived at the point in his life story where in 1961 he joined The Lincolns. That band—and the new friends he made—gave Frank's teenaged self a safe refuge where he could both protect and work out his identity as a young gay man. If you read what Frank has left us—along with John MacLachlan Gray's foreword—you will understand why Frank selected "appreciation" to sum up his feelings for what The Lincolns had given him. I salute you, Frank MacKay, for the courage and candour you express, and for the example you offer to others struggling today as you once did.

2019

On January 10, 2019, I sat down with Jay Johnston (the author of this book) to reminisce for a second time about The Lincolns, the extremely popular dance band I sang with during the 1960s. As we neared the end of that memory session, Jay asked me the following: "If you could use one word to describe what The Lincolns meant to you, what would it be?"

Without hesitating, I answered: "Appreciation."

I don't know whether it was the choice of response or the immediacy of reply, but from the look on his face I could see that further information was called for. I added the following: "I believe The Lincolns, as an entity, saved my life."

1956

Coming of age in a small town is difficult enough at the best of times, but if it was Small Town, North America, during the mid- to late 1950s and you just happened to be a bit "different," it could seem downright impossible. In my case, different meant "gay," and although that particular expression would eventually become the popular "go-to" word for describing the LGBT community in general, back when I was a kid it wasn't one of the ones I heard on a daily basis both inside and outside my home. Those words were usually vulgar and profane, and from what I could tell, almost always aimed at someone the users felt a huge disdain for.

It was around this time I knew I was keeping a "secret," one that if ever discovered would not only destroy me, but bring great dishonour on my family. To make sure that never happened, I went to war with myself. Quiet and reserved for the most part, I suddenly became a young "Mister Joviality" (on the outside, that is). Smiling, joking, the class clown, doing whatever it took to fit in. Meanwhile, (on the inside) it was all a lie. Experiencing thoughts and feelings that no one else in the world was experiencing? How could that be? And why was it only happening to me? I was in desperate need of someone to talk to. But who?

The answer to that question was...no one! The reason for this is that during this time period, if you scratched just below the surface of many small towns, you'd find prejudices, biases that had been held onto and passed down like family heirlooms. My own kin were no exception. With a trio of older brothers, and being four years younger than the last of the three, some of the things I'd hear coming out of their mouths at times were not only despicable sounding, but absolutely frightening to me. Especially when I was eleven or twelve and just beginning to come to grips with my own sexuality. It wasn't their fault, though, they had good teachers, who had good teachers, who had....

1981

In March of 1981, I was appearing at the National Arts Centre in Ottawa in the world premiere of John Gray's *Rock and Roll*, a very popular stage musical based on The Lincolns, when one night during the run I received a note at intermission from an old Truro school chum who was attending that evening's performance. The message said she was with a few other Truro locals, and they were all wondering if I might join them in the lobby after the show. I did and was surprised to find a dozen people amassed there, and since it was obviously an event waiting to happen I suggested we go upstairs to the bar, where we asked a waiter to put three tables side by side by side, so we could all sit together and continue our giddy little hometown gabfest. As is the case with many of these types of social occasions, after the first half-hour or so, the conversations have a tendency to break off into more "one on ones," which is exactly what happened to me and my friend, whom I shall call "Holly."

Holly and I had been classmates back in our junior high days at St. Mary's Catholic School in Truro, and so our own wee "tête-à-tête" began with inane stories about "Mother Saint This" and "Sister Saint That." As our discussion continued, however, I noticed that she kept bringing her late brother "Ted" into the mix.

Holly: "You remember Ted, don't you, Frank?"

Me: "Of course."

(I knew who Ted was, but I didn't know him well as he was a year or two older than both Holly and I. Ted had passed away in the mid-sixties under mysterious circumstances, and at the time there were those in town who hinted it had happened at his own hand. Getting a sense that Holly "really wanted to talk," I nodded at a couple of empty bar stools, to which she whispered a very appreciative "Thank you.")

Holly: "If only Ted knew this day was coming."

Me: "What do you mean?"

Holly: "Well, everything today is so open isn't it—for gay people, I mean."

(Thanks to 1970s TV sitcoms like *Soap*, where Billy Crystal's character was openly gay, and *Three's Company*, whose lead actor John Ritter played a straight man pretending to be gay, things in 1981 certainly seemed to be moving in the right direction acceptance-wise, although still not where it should have been.)

Holly: "You knew Ted was gay?"

Me: "No, I didn't."

Holly: "You heard what happened to him?"

Me: "There were rumours, Holly. But believe me, as a gay man who was lucky enough to survive the sixties, I can only imagine the pain Ted was going through to go that far."

Holly: "I saw him the afternoon before it happened, and it was like he was having a nervous breakdown or something. I tried to get him to tell me what was wrong, but each time I did, he would just bury his head in his hands. His behaviour was scaring me, and so I told him that if he wouldn't talk to me, please talk to Mom and Dad at least. 'Uh-uh!' he stammered. 'Uh-uh, Mom and Dad will never know.' Then looking at me with the greatest hurt I've ever seen in another's eyes, he shouted, 'Don't you go telling them either, you hear? Don't you go telling them!' And I didn't."

Me: "I'm sorry, Holly."

Holly: "About six months after Ted left us, I got a phone call from a friend of his, Ben. As soon as I heard the name I had an instant flashback to the last year of Ted's life and of how this Ben and he were inseparable. At the same time it hit me that I couldn't remember seeing him at the funeral, nor at any time since then, for that matter, which struck me as rather odd. Apparently Ben had something he wanted to talk to me about and was wondering if I might find a moment to meet with him. Although hesitant at first, I finally agreed, and we set a date for the next day at the park. The following afternoon I found Ben sitting on one of the swings in the area of the park we had chosen. As I got within earshot I heard him nervously half-stutter, 'Hi, Holly. Thank you for seeing me.' 'Ben,' I said tepidly.

"I could bore you with details of how we 'broke the ice' conversation-wise, but I'd rather jump right to what Ben had to say. It seems both he and my brother were outsiders who just happened to find each other through their mutual love of two things, bowling and comic books. I can vouch for the comics, as Ted's room was always littered with them. Because Ben had a part-time job that began mid-Saturday afternoon and took up most of his weekend, the two of them would often meet Saturday morning, bowl a couple of strings, and then lunch afterwards at the snack bar up the street. This one particular Saturday Ben noticed that Ted was acting very peculiar, like he wanted to say something but didn't know how to.

"After some playful teasing that went nowhere, Ben asked Ted point blank, 'All right, what's buggin' you? Whatever it is pal, spit it out.' After a couple of false starts Ted slowly began to tell Ben about the feelings he was having for him, and of how over the past couple of months they had become so strong he could no longer hold them in. 'You're joking, right?' Ben laughed.

"Answering honestly, Ted replied, 'I'm serious, Ben. I can't stop thinking about you.' At that moment, Ben said he was totally taken aback and felt as if he had been struck by a fear-filled thunderbolt. The only way he could deal with it was to go on the attack. The restaurant was nearly full, and with all eyes on the two of them, Ben went up one side of Ted and down the other. Leaving the diner, Ben yelled back at my brother, 'Never speak to me again.'

"'I miss Ted, Holly. I miss him every single day,' Ben blurted out in tears. 'Why? That's what I want to know, why was my initial reaction to strike out like that? Ted was my best friend. You're supposed to be there for your best friend, aren't you? And it's killing me, Holly, killing me that my behaviour might well have been what pushed him to do what he did. I know nothing would have changed between us that way, but if only we had talked. Maybe I'd still have a best friend, because I sure don't have one now.'

"'If only we had talked.' Ironic, wouldn't you say, Frank? Here it is 1981, and you and I are sitting at a bar in Ottawa speaking openly about something that a mere fifteen years ago was taboo."

(And with that, one of Holly's friends from the party tables invited us to join in a toast: "To Mushaboom and Truro!")

1957

In the summer of 1957 I moved from one small town to another small town, and although the surroundings were new, the groundings were not, and the "who am I" game continued for another two/three years. Until the fall of 1961, that is.

CHRONOLOGY

The Lincolns were—stealing Hemingway's term for Paris—something of a moveable feast, a moveable musical feast. Based on the information provided me, here is who was in the band at different times. I apologize to anyone I've missed.

The Valiants, 1959-60: Brian Chisholm, Peter Harris, Frank Mumford, Rod Norrie

The Lincolns, 1960-61: Brian Chisholm, Layne Francis, Frank MacKay, Frank Mumford, Rod Norrie

The Lincolns, 1962-64: Brian Chisholm, Layne Francis, Frank MacKay, Frank Mumford, Rod Norrie, Lee Taylor

The Lincolns on hold, 1964-65: From May 1964 to the summer of 1965, band members go their separate ways, Frank MacKay to Sarnia, Ontario

The New Lincolns, 1965: Layne Francis, Frank MacKay, Don Muir, Frank Mumford, Rod Norrie, Lee Taylor

The Lincolns, 1966–March 1968: Layne Francis, John MacLachlan Gray, Frank MacKay, Don Muir, Frank Mumford, Rod Norrie, Lee Taylor

The Lincolns, March–summer 1968: Layne Francis, Frank MacKay, Don Muir, Frank Mumford, Rod Norrie, Barry Ryan, Dick Snook

The Lincolns, summer 1968–spring 1969: Layne Francis, Charlie Gray, Jack Lilly, Frank MacKay, Don Muir, Frank Mumford, Barry Ryan, Dick Snook

The Lincolns, spring–September 1969: Layne Francis, Jack Lilly, Frank MacKay, Don Muir, Barry Ryan, Dick Snook, Gregg "Phisch" Fancy (for a month or so on bass), Don Morris (for several months on bass)

Occasional players/singers: John Hollis, Lawson Barkhouse, Bubs Brown, Bruce Jackson, Peter Cox

Road crew, 1968–69: James "Lukey" Maxwell, Frank Borden, Scott "Dinkles" Clyke

Stage crew, 1978 Reunion: Barry "Scrapper" Stevenson, Vernon Daley

Additional musicians at various Lincolns reunions between 1978 and 2019: Brian Chisholm, Gregg "Phisch" Fancy, Jeff Goodspeed, Dawn Hatfield, Glenn Irving, Shirley Jackson

1978: First reunion, fundraiser for minor football, at Nova Scotia Teachers' College

1979: Reunion at Colchester Stadium, Truro

1981: Premiere of John Gray's *Rock and Roll*

1985: *The King of Friday Night* broadcast on CBC TV

1990s–early 2000s: Reunion performances in Truro, Halifax, New Glasgow, and Tatamagouche

2003: Music Industry of Nova Scotia and the American Federation of Musicians (Local 571) recognize The Lincolns for their outstanding contribution to the Musical Legacy of the Province of Nova Scotia

2015: Colchester Historeum in Truro includes The Lincolns in its core exhibit

2016: Members of The Lincolns receive lifetime achievement awards from the Cobequid Arts Council for their contribution to the arts and cultural sector of the community

2017: Fundraiser for the Colchester Historeum, Truro

2018: "At the Legion—One Last Time," fundraiser for the Marigold Centre, September 14-15 performances that mark six unforgettable decades of The Lincolns

2019: Celebration of Life for Frank MacKay, held at the Marquee Club, Halifax, May 12, 2019

2020: With Charlie A'Court on vocals, The Lincolns perform at the Marigold Centre, Truro, May 9, 2020, to mark the launch of this book

ACKNOWLEDGEMENTS

A *great many people contributed to this book by sharing stories, images, and* other details. It all began with a phone call I received from Rod Norrie in August 2018, asking if I might be interested in telling the story of The Lincolns. You bet I was. Thank you, Rod. (And thank you Elinor Maher, my sister, for suggesting to Rod that I might be interested in such a project.)

I have a long list of people to thank, but first I have to say something about the main subjects of the book, the musicians in The Lincolns. Your performances moved me in the 1960s, and again at various reunion concerts decades later. Your recollections, shared in face-to-face interviews, phone calls, and emails, form the heart and soul of this book. Thank you a second time Rod Norrie, and equally Layne Francis, Don Muir, John MacLachlan Gray, Jack Lilly, Barry Ryan, Phisch Fancy, and Dick Snook for sharing some of what you lived.

Frank MacKay would have been in the preceding paragraph, but he passed away suddenly in early March 2019. Like everyone else who ever met Frank, I was stunned. He was not just larger than life, he seemed to be life itself. At seventy-four, he could still sing as he did at seventeen, maybe better. And in addition to his rich and powerful voice, Frank possessed more than any ordinary person's share of kindness and charisma. His willingness to sit down with me and talk about his life, and to respond to emailed questions, helped this book immeasurably. And when I asked him to write an afterword, Frank agreed right away. He saw it as an opportunity to share a long hidden and important story, one that could possibly help others.

Thank you, John MacLachlan Gray, for your piece that kicks off this book. It was shortly before Frank MacKay died that I asked him to consider writing something as a foreword. When Frank died about forty-eight hours later, John composed his moving tribute to his lost friend.

While stories from band members form the core of the book, I thought it important to have fan memories, too. And a few recollections from Frank MacKay's Sarnia bandmates and other musicians he had played with. Sometimes those individuals told me a lot, sometimes just a little. It all helped. In alphabetical order, here are the names of those people and institutions I wrote down as contributing in some way to this book: Charlie A'Court, Stephen Archibald, Jane Bailey, Joe Ballard, Renée Belliveau (Mount Allison University Archives), André Chiasson, Joan Chiasson (Dalhousie University Archives), John Chiasson, Mary Clancy, Helen Dorrington-Price, Tim Forbes, Dave Gass, Bob Grant, Tim Griffin, Dawn Hatfield, Brian Hill, Doug Hiltz, David R. Hubley, Joanne Hunt (Colchester Historeum), Charlotte Isnor, Colin Johnston, Danny Joseph, Christine Lovelace (University of New Brunswick Archives & Special Collections), Bob MacDonald, Winston MacDonald, Alex MacDougall, Sharon MacKay, Karen MacLean, Elinor Maher, David Mawhinney (Mount Allison University Archives), James "Lukey" Maxwell, Wayne Mont, Sam Moon, Glenn Morrison, Heather Mumford, Nancy Mumford, Ian Murray, Scott Murray, Wayne Nicholson, Jackie Norrie, Joy O'Brien, Sherry O'Brien-Stevens, Jud and Gay Pearson,

Nancy St. John Pond, Pridham's Studio, Gary Ramey, Rosaria Rovero, Lynn MacMurtery Schnare, Bryan Skinner, Craig Stanfield, Patricia Starratt, David States, Ashley Sutherland (Colchester Historeum), Colin Topshee, Mary Topshee, Maxine Wallace, and Doreen Woodworth. I also want to thank freelance copy editor Barry Norris, cover designer Colin Smith, and everyone at Nimbus Publishing, especially Angela Mombourquette and Jenn Embree, for steering the book through to publication.

In a category all their own go Eleanor Norrie and Sylvia Macdonald. Both were of tremendous assistance recalling events, finding photos and other source material, and locating people with stories I had not heard. Neither was in the band, yet each was a whole lot more than any ordinary fan. As a result, Eleanor and Sylvia get this paragraph all to themselves.

Another person who deserves a warm and appreciative acknowledgement is the Hon. Margaret Norrie McCain. The former lieutenant-governor of New Brunswick and chancellor of Mount Allison University thought that the many stories of the era of The Lincolns needed to be both preserved and told, and encouraged me to take it on. Thank you, Margie. Without you, this book would not exist.

I am grateful to one and all mentioned above, and express additional thanks to Mary Topshee. For over eight months you listened to me as I told you bits and pieces about The Lincolns, and not once did you say "That's enough." I appreciated that, as I do everything else you do in this life of ours.

A. J. B. (John) Johnston is the author or co-author of twenty-one books: sixteen on different aspects of the history of Atlantic Canada and five novels. The Canadian Historical Association awarded a Clio prize to his *Endgame 1758: The Promise, the Glory and the Despair of Louisbourg's Last Decade,* and *Ni'n na L'nu: The Mi'kmaq of Prince Edward Island* was selected in 2014 as the best published Atlantic book. John was made a chevalier of France's Ordre des Palmes académiques in recognition of his many publications on the French presence in Atlantic Canada. He lives in Halifax with his wife, Mary. For more information, please visit ajbjohnston.com.